THE ESSENTIAL PRINCIPLES OF
ED PARKER'S KENPO KARATE

LEE WEDLAKE

Copyright © 2025 Lee Wedlake

All rights reserved, including the right to reproduce this book, or portions thereof in any form. No part of this text may be reproduced, transmitted, downloaded, decompiled, reverse engineered, or stored, in any form or introduced into any information storage and retrieval system, in any form or by any means, whether electronic or mechanical without the express written permission of the author.

The views expressed in this work are solely those of the author and do not necessarily reflect the views of the publisher, and the publisher hereby disclaims any responsibility for them.

ISBN: 978-1-918038-38-5

PublishNation LLC
www.publishnation.net

TO DAD

Books by Lee Wedlake

The Kenpo Karate Compendium

Lee Wedlake's Kenpo Companion

Lessons with Ed Parker 2024

Further Insights into Kenpo

Kenpo Karate 101 through 601

Fiction with Phil Buck

Whisper From The Alamo

Runaway Blues

Life on Maui

Vimeo Website Training Videos

Lee Wedlake's Kenpo Karate – Beginner through Advanced Levels (Kenpo 101/201/301):
Vimeo.com/ondemand/kenpo101

Lee Wedlake's Kenpo 401 and Instructing for Instructors:
Vimeo.com/ondemand/kenpo401

Preface

In this book, Senior Master Wedlake sets forth Ed Parker's timeless concepts and principles of American Kenpo in a concise and easy to understand format. No one is more qualified than he to do this.

Understanding these principles and the thought processes that generated them cannot fail to greatly increase the knowledge and hence the effectiveness of Ed Parker's art for beginners and seasoned practitioners as well.

Gary Swan
Student of Kenpo

Sifu Swan is one of the most respected and influential practitioners of Kenpo, being not only a Senior Master and President of the National Chinese Kenpo Karate Association but also a certified acupuncturist, retired Command Sergeant Major (U.S. Army), firearms instructor and has taught in Universal City, Texas for over 50 years

Introduction

There's much more cross-training today than when I started in the arts in the late 1960s. Recently I had some of my black belts across the country who do Brazilian Jiu-Jitsu tell me a book on the 32 main principles of that art was published and that "we need something like that". My thinking is that while we do have that embedded in Ed Parker's writing, as well as my own, extracting them would be useful. So, here we go.

While principles of physics are not "Parker principles", being that they are universal, Ed Parker did emphasize elements of his art he specifically called principles. In my studies in arts other than Kenpo and in discussions with numerous instructors of various arts, I realized there are constants; principles that permeate systems of motion across the board. One Aikido instructor I met called them "Golden Threads". Another term I like is "Universal Truths". I believe one needs to understand and apply those because you live in a body and it is subject to the laws of physics. A few of these principles are spinal alignment, breathing and relaxation. There is an excellent book on the physics of the martial arts entitled *Parting the Clouds* by Grenville Harrop. Now, on to the Parker principles.

There is a difference in concepts and principles. Ed Parker had ideas on application of his art (concepts) and when these proven they became the principles of Kenpo Karate. Some instructors in our art dispute there are "rules" in our system yet I submit there are. Call them guidelines, or highly recommended, whatever term you like. Just as in language we have rules, rules that get bent from time to time such as "I before E except after C" in the English language, Kenpo has rules of motion. This is hardly unique. It is what makes systems different, they have their rules of motion. One of my early teachers, Mike Sanders, said "If Tae Kwon Do people did with their hands what they do with their feet, they'd be Kenpo." I've seen TKD people use their feet like hands, so I agree.

Ed Parker was credited by the late John Corcoran with being the first to create a glossary of terminology for the martial arts. He replaced esoteric names for posture and movement with Western terms. His labeling of concepts and principles has been borrowed by many outside our system, often along with adopting the application for their own use. I have been often told "I'm going to use that" by non-Kenpo instructors when I show or describe the ideas. This book should give you insight into the Parker thinking and some hows and whys for our instructional methods and applications. I remember being in the car with Mr. Parker and he made a comment that "It could be said that I know everything", based on his extensive knowledge of motion. That didn't mean he knew every system, he meant he knew movement and application. I thought that was a very interesting statement.

These are in no particular order. I have roughly grouped them in related categories and labeled them as Structural, Conceptual and Application. I wrote this with newer students in mind but black belts will get some nuggets from this as well. The main headings indicate what I thought are important to know and I included other related principles and terms. There is overlap, with reference to other chapters since nothing really stands on its own, so the heading is the main idea. I originally did not intend it to be a "how-to" execute a technique or a "how-to" teach but that material worked in and it may also be helpful for instructors and those who aspire to be. So, you'll find some psychology, anatomy, pedagogy and other helpful information. I think you'll enjoy the stories.

As stated above that nothing stands on its own, we have to consider the integration of not only these physical principles but the mental and emotional facets. I include some of the thinking and psychological elements related to fighting in the chapters but have also added a section by Gary Ellis, of Plymouth, England, one of the first black belts promoted in Europe by Mr. Parker in 1980. The symbolism of the marrying of the Tiger and Dragon are embedded in our system and Gary points them out relative to the Warrior Mindset and its development through progressive study and movement.

Acknowledgments

I thank all my teachers and my father in every book, as well as those who helped in the production in a variety of ways, and my students who supported me over the years. Mike Sanders was one of my first teachers and really opened my eyes to the arts. Ed Parker took me under his wing and that provided opportunities to learn from Frank Trejo, one of the best in our system, with outstanding talents in fighting, forms and self-defense. He was running the headquarters school in Pasadena, California and he had me teaching there when I was in town. I worked with Sibok Tom Kelly, Mr. Parker's right-hand man, the late Richard "Huk" Planas, who was the State of the Art instructor for the IKKA, and Joe Palanzo, rated in forms and fighting. Being part of the Parker organization got me introduced to black belts such as knife-maker Gil Hibben, top coach and fighter Bob White, Gary Swan, Sigung Steve LaBounty (who was instructor to Tom Kelly, Gary Swan and Huk Planas) and Ron Chapel. I'd meet those who would become my peers along the way, such as John Sepulveda, Brian Duffy, Dennis Conatser, Skip Hancock, Paul Mills, and more. Still others were junior to me and would go on study with me and keep the flame burning, those being Gary Ellis, Graham Lelliott, and Steve White. I have long-time students "in the trenches" teaching for years and others developing add-on specialties to the system, some of those being Kurt Barnhart, Steve Hatfield, Bruce Meyer, Ed Cabrera and Phil Buck. You'll read in this book about no one principle standing alone and so it is with teaching the art. These people, and many more, have been there to keep Parker Kenpo alive and I salute them all.

I credit Danny Sullivan of Covington, Louisiana, as well as Rick Vecchi and Dan Helie of Chicago for their help with posing for photos.

My thanks to Phil Buck for doing the cover art.

Table of Contents

Preface V
Introduction.. VII
Acknowledgments IX

Structural Principles 1
    Body alignment and bracing angles 3
    Setting your base is Rule #1 8
    Open-ended triangles 9
    Three Dimensions, Three Power Principles 12

Conceptual Principles 13
    The Considerations of Combat 15
    Flexibility in thought and action 17
    The Four Ranges of Parker Kenpo 18
    Master Key principle 21
    Three Points of View 23
    Embryonic to Sophisticated Basics 25
    Universal Pattern 26
    Web of Knowledge/Family Groupings 27
    Point of origin/reference 31
    Overkill vs Over-skilled 31

Application Principles 33
    Stages of learning, variable expansion and more 35
    Margin for Error 37
    Checking 39
    White and Black Dot Focus 41
    Multiple attackers 42
    Footwork... 49
    The Four Ts - Tools, Timing, Targets and Travel 52
    Purposeful compliance and purposeful defiance 55
    Speed/Explosiveness 56
    Minors/majors 65
    Tailoring 66
    "With" vs "And then"... 68
    Contouring 69
    Weapon principles.. 71
    Thoughts on the combat mindset by Gary Ellis, 10TH degree 73

Structural Principles

Body alignment and bracing angles

There is no argument that alignment is key. Try straight punching with a bent wrist.

Figure 1: Punching with bent wrist.

This should prove to you that the proper alignment of the wrist is vitally important. We call this a bracing angle. One of the Golden Threads is triangulation of the body. The typical forward stance creates a bracing triangle in the lower body. Braces anticipate impact, both giving and receiving. Various systems position feet differently, the most common versions are front foot straight, back foot on an angle and another is front foot on the angle and back foot straight (which is what Parker Kenpo and few others systems do). Both accomplish the same goal. Triangulation is evident in the structure of the punching hand and arm as well as how the punch is the point of a triangle. Ignoring this alignment usually results in reduced effect and possible injury to self.

Figure 2: Good triangulation

Figure 3: Good alignment

You must align yourself efficiently while you disturb or destroy the opponent's alignment. We call this "breaking the waist". For the practitioner, it is what your teacher stressed - hips and shoulders in line. You just plain hit harder when they are. Conversely, a groin kick gets the opponent to bend either from the impact, pain or just moving the lower body away to avoid being struck. The broken waist prevents or diminishes their ability to align correctly to counter because the hips and shoulders are now out of line.

Figure 4: Poor alignment

Figure 5: Broken waist

Knee and ankle alignment. Watch to see that your knee bends over your instep, activating the hinge as is intended. Too often we see knees flexing laterally (outward and inward) instead of forward and back. This can been seen in improper shifts to a forward bow stance. It's common and doing that can cause a repetitive stress injury to the knee. A seasoned teacher needs to point it out to newer instructors as it can be a bit hard to detect. Something just doesn't look right but once you see it, you've got it. When in a twist stance or kneel, the rear ankle, as an example, should be vertical. The heel and the ball should align; after all, it's weight-bearing. The foot being on an angle is often seen, which is poor alignment and can cause injury and loss of balance. It stresses the ankle and knee joints too.

Level shoulders and hips. Generally, your hips and shoulders should be parallel with the floor or ground. There are exceptions, such as fighting on a slope or rolling and pitching ship deck (which Ed Parker was known to do). Having one side higher than the other affects center of gravity, energy management (momentum) and the energy used in muscle engagement could probably be better used elsewhere. Having an erect carriage from the top of the head down is important. Hunching your shoulders and rolling up your back like a boxer works but you have to be in great shape to sustain that position. Raising one shoulder seems to be common in Kenpo people for some reason. Listen to your teacher when they correct that or watch video of yourself and work on it.

Elbows anchored. California Kenpo black belt, Howard Silva, said "When your elbows are in, you'll win. When they're out, there's some doubt." I love that saying. Ed Parker defined anchoring as weighting your elbows and your buttocks, for margin for error, protection and economy of motion. Dropping your hips helps stability. Having your elbows out won't cover your ribs, they can be struck and you'd have to re-align them to throw an effective strike.

Body alignment affects breathing. Having your head erect, "head-top suspended", aligns the spine from head to heel, provided your hips are tucked in, as they should be. Letting your chin drop restricts breathing. Take a deep breath with your head up, then drop your chin as far as you can and take a deep breath. You'll feel the restriction when the chin is down. Breath is life and being able to use as much of your lung capacity helps with endurance, among other things. Unfortunately, in today's world, the chin-down posture is the most-used by people on their phones. You should be breathing with your diaphragm, which is frequently called "belly breathing". Lay on your back, put your hand on your belly and you should feel it rise and sink. If you breathe with your chest, you won't.

Ed Parker made an analogy to a teapot in regard to breathing. When the water in the teapot boils with the lid on, the escaping steam whistles from the spout. It has pressure being relieved. Take the lid off and the whistle stops, the pressure being dissipated and its energy dispersed. He wanted us to focus that energy release with our breath to enhance power. The kiai, the sharp shout we use does this. It's "hi-ya" or something like it, not "hiiiiiii-yaaaaaaa". Without the kiai, we still use the breath for the same reasons. It links mind, body and spirit. (Kiai translates as "harmonize energy", or spirit shout.) Parker's definitions state unification of mind, breath, body and spirit for power development and application. A pressure cooker comes to mind. The pressure must be regulated to be effective or it explodes. Your breath must do the same and he liked to use what he called incremental breathing. Since we so often do multiple moves, unlike many systems which often do a 1-2 combination, you release the breath in increments, with the major moves coupled with the appropriate breath increment. A four move combination might have four exhalations. You wouldn't do a lengthy combination with one long breath, the previously described hiiiiiii-yaaaaaaa. You get the picture. Exhaling also stabilizes the body and tenses the core for protection of the internals as well. You don't want to get hit when you're holding your breath or breathing in. It's uncomfortable. Align yourself properly, relax when and where prescribed, use the diaphragm, time the movements properly and kiai – internally or externally.

It's important to stay relaxed. Tensing prematurely when striking reduces speed and power. Ed Parker had an interesting term for this, which was "constipated motion". That tension affects breathing. It may also cause you to carry your shoulders too high, using energy and constricting motion. Shawn and Rebecca Knight, two black belts I teach in Tucson, Arizona phrase it as "Swimming through chunky peanut butter". In Tai Chi, one is told to relax, and sink. Other movement disciplines emphasize relaxation, often in a supine position. I believe this is because you can't truly relax when standing as it takes some muscle engagement to simply stand up. I met a Marine Gunnery Sergeant when I attended a firearm instructor course. He asked me if I thought standing was complex muscle movement. He said that when he was in a firefight in Vietnam he reacted by falling to his knees, and later observed numerous other troops do the same. It wasn't that is was what was taught but a reaction to stress. Based on that, he believed it is a complex movement. This addresses the thought that you can't truly relax in a standing position. I leave it to those with more knowledge and experience to decide what they think.

Relaxation is not only physical but the mind and emotions need to be relaxed. I write of this elsewhere in this book. Parker's flexibility in thought and action is cogent, as is controlling emotions in combat.

Consider relaxation in the opponent as well. I was told if you want to get the other guy to relax, hit him real hard. As established, tension in the body is required to stand and move. Remove the tension, those abilities are reduced or eliminated. We know that folding up or dropping is a reaction to a hard, effective strike. Therefore, I agree.

Setting your base is Rule #1

Setting your base, also known as solidifying your base, was something Mr. Parker emphasized. He'd adjusted, over time, the stances to be higher than what he taught in the early days, which now allowed better mobility but low enough the base was solid. We call this Rule #1 – Set Your Base.

Careful observation of motion will reveal that it's an often ignored rule. You'll see a foot lifted in transition to a stance, then set down. The problem here is contact. If you're grabbed, with a rear choke for example, and you lift your foot, you are on one-point balance. That's precarious. If you're turning to face behind as you do so, what are you using to support the movement? We were taught to establish the base first. The reason, I suspect, that practitioners don't do this is because they think it's faster. Which it is, by microseconds. But it does not use the principles he emphasized. He told us that the first step was most often used to 1) establish your base, 2) disturb his base (when you're grabbed because you're connected and your motion pulls him off balance, 3) generate body momentum, 4) control/cancel their zones and 5) reduce your exposure (blading, turning sideways, or whatever term you like).

Slide your foot/feet for two-point ground contact (no "jet lag"), drop your weight by bending your knees (flexing your ankles, depending), use that ground contact to determine what the surface is or of there is an obstruction of some sort (a wall, maybe). Under stress you may experience tunnel vision and reading that ground contact could be critical. Relax and breathe.

Many of the techniques use a "Pin, step, hit" concept. Pin the offending hand, slide your foot to establish the base, and hit. It does not have to be 1-2-3, the "space between the notes" can be very short. Think 1 with 2, then strike. This is a general rule. You may not pin, but the idea is to check. And checking can be by position among other ways. So maybe you think "Check, step, hit".

A related idea is to consider that if you are dropping back on a particular strike, look to see if you're backing away from the strike versus sinking down. There's a difference. We see people backing up as they strike, so their mass is not properly engaged. Once again, if you're moving too fast, you may be doing just that. As we say, Speed Kills. Speed kills power, in this instance. However, you do need to know that the physics formula tells us that when you double mass, you double power. When you double speed, you quadruple power. But if your body is moving in the wrong direction, or not enough or at all, you lose that.

Open-ended triangles

This is a critical principle used throughout the system. As defined in his *Infinite Insights into Kenpo, Vol. 5*, he wrote, "Refers to the positioning of your body parts so that they form an open-end triangle. Use of these body formations help to funnel, wedge, trap, or prevent an opponent from injuring you."

The principle is introduced early in beginner self-defense techniques. It carries through and, I believe, is key to understanding the margin for error positions therein, especially in the weapon defenses. I had done Filipino Martial Arts and worked with their "knife-tapping" drills, which emphasize the use of what we call the open end triangle. When I connected that with what Mr. Parker had been telling us, it expanded my thinking and understanding of what he was doing. In his lessons he had repeatedly talked about the open end triangle and how important it was. However, I never saw him demonstrate how it facilitated transitions between techniques of weapon defense. That was an aspect of his teaching method I was aware of, that he'd tell you about or allude to something and would wait to see if you figured it out. That's good, and bad. It's good because, as he said, "If you have to pull teeth to get the answer, it sticks, it means more." It's bad because if you don't, you go along thinking you have it when you really don't. You only have a part. When I have shown others those transitions and the linkage between the techniques, their eyes light up and understanding occurs.

One of the first examples I like is *Attacking Mace*. The right punch attack is blocked with your left inward block. Your right is chambered at the ribs because you've canceled their width zone to prevent the left punch follow-up being that you're outside the attack and you want full travel for your next move, the straight right punch to the ribs. There's another rule used here is outside, block above the elbow. Inside, block below the elbow. Above means toward the body. That becomes obvious when you compare this to *Delayed Sword*. That technique is inside the attack and makes contact below the elbow, which is a hinge. If you contact the elbow at or above it, the hinge can activate and the hand comes around the block, which necessitates having your check up. Being outside, the hinge can't move the same way, and allows the chamber of the right hand. When the punch is delivered, the left hand maintains position as a pressing check and this creates the open-end triangle. What you do from there depends on their reaction but the position has created a margin for error position.

Figure 5: The elbow is checked, preventing its bending.

In the intermediate level, *Swinging Pendulum* is taught as a defense against a roundhouse kick. It introduces the Universal Block, which is a double block executed as simultaneous inward and downward blocks. They create the open-end triangle shape, the open side being the side where the kick is met. Again, it's margin for error because combination kicks often rely on one falling for the fake and being open for the follow-up. The block provides a larger area of coverage. In addition, this technique is the first example (in the original curriculum) of moving up the circle to defend against a roundhouse kick. That movement is done earlier in two techniques to give you reach and give a good entry angle for an application. What's being taught here is not only that but that we always move away from the apex of a roundhouse kick to dissipate its impact, but it sets a bracing angle. You'll see this again in at least two later techniques. This rule gets broken when people change the intended attack in *Bowing to Buddha,* a kick defense in Form Four, that is done in a kneeling position. The technique is for a front kick. When done for a roundhouse, they don't move up the circle and they change the block to what basically is an extended outward with the left. There is no bracing angle, as you are on a 12-6 line and the force is entering on the 3-9 line. When I discuss this with those who learned it for a roundhouse kick, I ask them if that's how they would prefer to handle a Muay Thai roundhouse kick to their head while on their knee and they have all declined. This is a great subject to experiment with in the What-If for that attack.

Figure 6: Open-ended triangle.

Thrusting Lance is a knife defense that was taught in the original green belt level. The open end triangle is created on the first move. It's intended to be done with a Universal Block type movement, the left hand low and done as a parry or parrying block inside the attacking right hand, and the right hand executed as a hammering inward to the radial nerve. It's not a 1 then 2 timing, they're not simultaneous but almost. The knife is a versatile weapon, which was why Ed Parker placed them at the top of the threat list in Form Six. He considered them as the most deadly, with clubs being next and guns last. A gun has to be pointed at the target, knives and clubs do not. That requires the most margin for error and the open-end triangle give us that. This technique is in Form Six and relating it to the others, one can see the value of transitions from one attack line to another and how the trap or funnel action of the configuration will help us survive.

The open-ended triangle exemplifies his thinking on checking, margin for error and mostly, his ideas of white and black dot focus. He loved to mess with our heads and would ask, "How many corners of a triangle?" Note he said "of" and not "in". While most responded with three, he countered with six, those being the inside and outside of each corner. His point was to get us to really look at something familiar differently.

Three Dimensions, Three Power Principles

When I started studying with Ed Parker he used the term "body momentum" a lot. He'd use the others I'll describe here but I remember he seemed to prefer body momentum. He bound the three dimensions of height, width and depth to the three major power principles. Torque was correlated to width. Back-up mass was correlated to depth. Marriage of Gravity (a.k.a. gravitational marriage) was correlated with height.

Torque. I took a Power Machine Technology course in college and torque was defined as twisting force and still is. A popular term used by Kenpo people is "rotational torque" and every engineer I've asked about that agrees you can't have torque without rotation on a given angle, so the term is redundant. You twist to generate it, whether by rotating your arm to punch or your body to block or strike.

That means your width zones change and it's why he related the width zone to the power principle.

Back-up mass. Body weight moving in line with the strike is the best definition I've heard. That means it can move forward (push power) or back (pull power). Shuffling in with a kick or punch uses push power. Stepping back, such as with an inverted hooking back-knuckle to the head when grabbed in a front bear-hug uses pull power.

Gravitational marriage. This is back-up mass on the vertical plane. The fact that it adds weight assisted by gravity makes the difference. A karate-ka I knew in college said you hit harder going down with gravity. We just have a name for that. Like an airplane, it takes more power to climb and a lot less to descend since we go with gravity instead of against.

When we ask a student what the power principle that is used in a technique or move, we really ask what the main one is. None of the power principles are independent of the others. When you punch in a horse stance, the primary principle is torque (assuming you're doing a basic straight punch, there are "natural punches" that don't twist). However, your arm is in motion which means there is an element of back-up mass, the weight of the arm behind the fist. So there are two power principles used in this example but torque is the primary. Analyzing motion in techniques, one will we often use three principles at once, which really maximizes power. The *Encyclopedia of Kenpo* has multiple terms describing this.

Conceptual Principles

The Considerations of Combat

This has been covered in his *Infinite Insights into Kenpo* books and my own but it needs to be included here. Please note that it was eight considerations when he published them in 1970 in the *Accumulative Journal*. By 1987 with the publication of *Infinite Insights into Kenpo Vol. 5* it was up to 11. I refer you to that book. Whichever model you use, they're both good. They show the Parker thinking of progressive degrees of importance and concept/principle groupings.

I read a book by Canadian psychologist, Dr. Jordan Peterson, who wrote that the "motivated animal" is aware of the "ever-present possibility of threat". In my opinion, we are motivated animals. If we're out in public, or even in our home, we realize something may occur that has to be handled one way or another. He goes on to state there is "risk and opportunity". In our world, risk may be presented by a physical attack, as an example, and target openings would present opportunity.

A situation has developed and a response is now required. There's a force progression you should follow and it starts with presence. Don't look like prey, be alert. Use verbal skills to de-escalate an altercation when you can't leave. Your mind is your greatest weapon. Parker's glossaries include terms related to psychological strategies. These should be thought out in advance. Run scenarios in your mind. What would I do if? Be sure to visualize successful outcomes. If you do have to physically respond, know that the law will be on your side to a point, or should be. The reasonable person standard will apply in court and knowing the force progression may be critical. You can break an arm, but do you have to? Did you have to gouge an eye out? Did you really have to do *Leap of Death* on a man who grabbed your lapel? Police and security officers are taught the progression starts with presence, then verbal skills, soft hands, hard hands, non-lethal weapons, then lethal weapons. Soft hands are making contact but not up to striking, which are the hard hands. If that's not enough, go to a baton, taser, pepper spray and the like. That's non-lethal. Lethal is use of a firearm to end the situation. It's hard to justify jumping from presence to lethal force without justification and people get arrested for that.

Acceptance is the first consideration, and it was added later, so it's really the Nine Considerations of Combat. You accept that you may need to defend yourself or loved ones and have thought about possible responses. You decided on how to train for it and that includes training in de-escalation tactics (verbal judo), martial arts or some form of weapon training. And you should have determined if you'll actually apply what you know. I met a woman who said if she was attacked by a rapist, she would not fight back, saying she'd let him do what he wanted. I was astonished. Had she considered he may rape and then kill her? There was no discussion, she'd made up her mind.

There are psychological after-effects of violence, up to and including taking life. I found the following on an internet forum. I'd been told of it in bodyguard school as something to be aware of should we shoot/kill someone.

Mark of Cain Syndrome: Important events change us and have great psychological importance for a time after they occur. In the case of a violent encounter there is a tendency to believe that whatever you were is irrelevant, that the only thing important in your life is that you hurt or killed someone. There's a reason police officers go on administrative leave after a shooting. You can't "play karate" in threatening situations.

Environment
It's what's on you, around you and in you. What you wear, your immediate surroundings, and your physical condition/mental state constitute environment.

Range
What's the distance between you and the opponent(s)? Distance equals time and time gives you opportunity to makes decisions.

Position
Are you standing and how? Passive, hands up position or fighting stance? One says (or seems to) that you don't want to fight, the other does not. Lying down?
Sitting at a desk or in a restaurant? In bed with the covers on? Your responses will be dictated by these factors.

Maneuvers
What movement is possible from these positions with foot, body or both?

Targets
What areas are available to be struck with what weapons?

Natural weapons
If you're in bed with the covers over you, kicking is not a likely option. Targets and weapons overlap here.

Blocks
As written in another section, it's footwork that usually keeps you from getting hit but in our bed scenario, blocking with the arms may be your only option.

Cover
You need to make distance between yourself and the attacker.

In his model using eleven considerations he ties in physical and mental conditioning as well as breathing and tailoring movement to the individual.

Flexibility in thought and action

In Jay T. Will's 1977 book, *Kenpo Karate for Self-Defense*, page 19 in the section titled "What is Kenpo?" has a quote from Ed Parker which goes; "It's flexible in thought and action and is formulated as encounters occur." This has a lot of rich meaning and I use it frequently. Mr. Parker told me a story about this quote, saying Will had called him on the telephone and asked him to describe the system. What would later be published in Will's book was a transcript of a recording of the conversation, which Mr. Parker said he did not know was being made. He was upset because he said he planned to use that very description in his *Infinite Insights into Kenpo* book, which would later become a series of volumes.

We need structure in so many things and a system does that for us. You might call some of those things routines yet I see them as systematic. It gets the job done but it should looked at from time to time to see if it can be done differently, with a better result. When we get so focused on that system or routine that we can't break out of it, that may be a problem. We observe that someone, maybe ourselves, is Obsessive Compulsive. It just has to be done a certain way. That is the opposite of flexibility in thought and action. It's easy to get into a rigid routine with the techniques, requiring that the pattern always be completed the same way, every time. Yes, it's important to learn and do the techniques and forms as prescribed to learn the concepts and principles embedded in them. It's like learning the alphabet and rules of language. You must have a command of such things before you modify them or you can modify yourself out of the system. And so it is with Kenpo. Yes, you must also practice in such a way as to develop the ability to adapt to changing situations. That's the flexibility he spoke of.

You need to do some thinking. What if I did this instead of that? Can I chop instead of punch? Must it be to the same target? And will the result be the same or similar? If so, I can continue with the pattern. If not, what would I have to do differently? You'll often find another technique or portion of one that meets the need of that change. That gives insights into how brilliantly he constructed the system.

The Four Ranges of Parker Kenpo

There are four ranges codified by Ed Parker, those being out of contact, in contact, contact penetration and contact manipulation.

Out of contact. (I remember him using out-of-range as the term but the books use "contact". Using contact would keep all the terms consistent.) No opponent can make contact, with a natural weapon, in this context.

In contact. (Again, I remember him saying in-range. I think you can be in range but not in contact.) The term, critical distance, is used here. It is, as defined by Parker, is the distance you can strike or be struck.

Contact penetration. The distance you can expect to get the desired result of your strike. Different weapons get different results. Some weapons, like an eye slice, skim the target yet get the planned result. Other weapons penetrate deeply, like a liver punch. The Russian Systema people like to say, "Skin, muscle, organ" when talking about depth of penetration. I like that.

Contact manipulation. This refers primarily to the stand-up jiu-jitsu aspect of Kenpo. Read the histories of the Kenpo systems in Hawai'i and you'll see the influence of Prof. Henry Okazaki and his Danzan-Ryu system on what we and others do. Many of the Parker techniques teach joint locking defense and application. Beginners learn how to apply a wrist lock and escape it as well. Advanced techniques teach how to do what many would call a lock-flow. They are done on both standing and downed opponents. (I think of striking as a form of contact manipulation because you get the body to react.)

All of this is tied into his Dimensional Zone Theory. He broke it down, starting with the basic Zone of Defense, which is the imaginary square in front of the body with four quadrants, like a window pane (an analogy used by many instructors of various arts). See his *Infinite Insights into Kenpo* books for detailed illustrations (keeping in mind he admitted the drawings were incorrect in places and would have to be re-done in the future), I don't want to be repetitive. What's not in the book is how deep that zone is. We measure it by folding an arm like an elbow strike and placing our fist on our sternum with the elbow to 12:00. I tell students it's like erecting a fence around your yard. You only really need to be concerned with what's entering the yard, not what's outside the fence. This zone gives us a starting point to get into the other zone ideas.

The Outer Rim is an egg-shaped area that provides us the latitude to go outside that box we created. Upward and extended outward blocks do so. I was totally unfamiliar with the concept when he first told me of it. It was 1978 at a tournament. I always asked the judges of my forms division what I could do to improve. He was the center judge. He told me I had gone out of "the egg-shaped perimeter", needed to condense movement and my stances were too low. I nodded my head, thinking I understood, but I really didn't. Egg-shaped perimeter? Never heard of it and he was occupied with others so I couldn't ask more. My initial Kenpo training did not include principles, terminology, intended applications and more. I thought the shape was visualized from front to back with the large part at my body and narrow part at the extended hands. I was thinking it was perpendicular to what he actually meant. I'd never been told I was over-extending, so maybe he just needed to say something. When I got home and told my new instructor, Mike Sanders, who was back-filling what I needed from my initial training with a sub-standard instructor about the stances he said "That #!$%. He always wanted a low horse." No comment about the Outer Rim, though. I think this illustrates two things. Ed Parker was always thinking and re-thinking, resulting in tweaks to the system. One was tailoring stances and that resulted in stances being done higher than what was originally taught, which was the era Mike learned them. Second, the terminology was not developed until the late 1960s and was first printed in the *Accumulative Journal*. * That meant many of the early generation probably didn't get the terms unless they stuck around. If you talk with those who were brown belts back then you'll be told they remember being shown the "new" material and given the terms, post 1970. I was fortunate that in 1979 I became a direct student of Mr. Parker and was taught these things and able to discuss them with him. Huk Planas told me he was the guinea pig in using the terms. Mr. Parker would sit and read the term to him to see if it got Huk to do what he intended.

Height, width and depth zones are described. I remember asking him why he detailed them as he did versus what other systems used, he said "That's how it looks to me". Was he arbitrarily setting the dividing lines to be different? Maybe, but it's his system and he could do what he wanted. So, we have three height zones, four width zones and eight depth zones. The zones are associated with two different terms for the <u>same area</u>, those being named by perspective, that is, the Horizontal Zone of Protection (or defense) and the Horizontal Zones of Attack. The depth zones were described in the *Accumulative Journal* as "It entails the protection of approximately four to six basic depth zones".

By the time Vol. 4 of *Infinite Insights into Kenpo* was published, it changed to seven depth zones. He'd later add the Obscure Zone to the total.

None of this really makes a difference if they're out of range. Once one or both of you are in range, it does. Available targets and use of natural weapons are dependent on what zones are presented. Trying to hit the chest squarely on a person who is angled dictates using a roundhouse weapon, for example, to hit it. The width zone is partially closed when viewed from the front. He viewed the width zones as being like a set of Venetian (his term, now usually called vertical) blinds on a window. They open and close to varying degrees. A person who bends or turns in any direction will cause the zones to change. Bending forward or back changes the dimensions of the horizontal zones. Dropping to the knees or going to the ground changes height. On the ground other zones are affected. He wanted us to look at those changes within the ideal phase techniques.

How deeply you follow through into a zone constitutes contact penetration. Some strikes we use skim the target, such an an eye slice. Others have more magnitude than a slice and are considered to be raking strikes. Ripping and tearing are related to those and incorporate elements of the others; "Tear his ear off", which would indicate you'd have to grab and pull. It could be torn off without a grab, though. And your good old straight punch to the ribs that one feels all the way inside is a great example of maximum contact penetration.

Contact manipulation is what you primarily do when you are in position to lock a joint(s). Parker's definition is "Control over your opponent, once contact is made. You may contour, leverage, takedown, restrain, twist, sprain, lock, dislocate, choke, etc. in order to increase the effectiveness of your action."

Locks are done by bending, straightening or twisting. A wrist lock is an example of bending, as are neck and spine locks. The spine is a series of joints and bending it in a variety of ways constitutes a lock. We also lock by straightening an arm or leg, often leading to a break. Twisting is often used in conjunction with bending and straightening, often as a compounding move. Contact manipulation is not limited to joint locking. You may have grabbed clothing and push or pull someone into position, the clothes being a handle. You're manipulating the body. Mr. Parker again looked at duration and magnitude when breaking down movement. For example, he saw pulling, yanking and jerking as being degrees of the same action. Pulling might be seen as more steady, while jerking and yanking are shorter, sharper moves. It's no surprise we have a lot of locking in our system when you think about the influence of Professor Okazaki and his Danzan-Ryu jiu-jitsu (which also had Lua components) on Hawaiian martial arts.

Locks happen when they happen. It's difficult to lock when you get too focused on locking. If it's there, take it. If it's not, continue with the striking, checking, etc. Every lock has a key and you're told the best way to get out of a lock is not to get into a lock. We teach locking defenses to not only show a way to escape but for students to learn to apply a lock correctly. This concept applies to every attack in every technique, the attack has to be applied with correct mechanics. In Kenpo, we refer to <u>free</u> and <u>perpetual control</u> techniques. Free techniques like *Five Swords* are done with a hand making contact, then leaving to go elsewhere. Techniques involving the aforementioned bending and twisting, like *Dominating Circles* use perpetual control.

Master Key principle

Today there are three divisions to the Master Key concept. There is a Master Key basic, a Master Key move, and a Master Key technique. Just as a master key opens many locks, a master key in Kenpo provides solutions to many different attacks. Ed Parker said that his teacher, William K. S. Chow, gave him the master keys.

A basic is a singular move. A Master Key basic is one that works for multiple applications. An inward block, (primitive stage) when thought of as simply an inward block, is not a Master Key. If you think of it as a raking back-knuckle to the face in the course of doing the block, it's a Master Key. This incorporates the double-factor idea.

When combining basics, it's now a Master Key move. Double block sequences like inward to outward are examples. Stepping forward and settling into a stance is singular. Making contact with their leg and buckling it while raking the nose and blocking, that's a Master Key move. Two basics at once.

A Master Key technique is a sequence that works for a variety of attacks without a change. Many of our techniques work for several attacks, often on the same line or situation. A defense for a straight punch inside the attack can also be used for a:

- Roundhouse punch
- Attempted grab (one or both arms)

- Attempted push (one or both arms)
- Completed grab
- Attempted kick

That's the basis of the idea. You don't have to choose between techniques. Once you're in the Point of Reference position, you do whatever is needed (formulation). The various techniques show you options. You can block, then chop or block, then kick.

There's criticism of Kenpo and other systems that have a lot of techniques. The argument is that since there are so many choices that it takes longer for a choice to be made. It's called Hicks' Law or Hick-Hyman Law. I've written about this in other books. It's an argument that doesn't really apply. If a punch is thrown, training gets you to respond, hopefully appropriately. You step to avoid, probably block or parry, then counter. You work inside, outside, over or under the attack, which is four possibilities. If it's an overhead punch, you eliminate over the arm because it's not practical and you would not go through a thought process to tell yourself not to do that. Your training, which incorporated see such attacks, recognizing the angles and answering, ingrained that already. Now you're down to three options, those being inside, outside or under. In our example, I can't see us going inside unless we're forced (environment, maybe), so now we're down to two. Outside or under the attack are our options. So it's really only two options and your body is in position to counter with given weapons to given targets based on the drills (techniques) you learned (those other options). We call it position recognition and we formulate as needed. To refute the Hick's Law argument, I say we have a smaller amount of initial options to choose from, thus speeding the decision process. You find yourself in a familiar position (whole body or maybe just a free limb) and respond. The Parker system lists 154 standard, ideal phase self-defense techniques but if you analyze them, there's really a handful of Point of Reference/Points of Origin we move from. Once again, the techniques are ideas and instructional methodology gets you to the level where you can spontaneously apply a technique or formulate your own.

Three Points of View

Simply put, they are yours, the opponent's and the bystander(s).

We, as the defender, have a unique viewpoint. The attacker's is totally different and unique as well. The third person, a bystander, can see things the first two may not. If you've been to a karate tournament and sat in the stands to watch a fight, you have probably seen a point scored that not one judge or referee seemed to see. No calls, no flags. That's the third person perspective. I was fighting in the brown belt division and my opponent threw a back-knuckle that should have been a point. We both hesitated, knowing it should have been called and it wasn't. We nodded our heads, smiled and resumed the match. We saw something the bystanders did not. I have to say he was fast - that fast. Enough that nobody else saw it.

Mr. Parker urged us to look at all three perspectives. You analyze the given technique with its application. You look for cancellation angles to prevent the back-up weapon from reaching you. You should then look at the attack side, for the same reason. Being the attacker, you should see what you might be able to do to counter or follow up in the course of the technique. You'll be better off doing this with a partner. I tell students to help each other find gaps, without being malicious, by attempting to strike, kick, buckle, take-down, etc. It's called co-operative opposition. Some call it pressure-testing the technique. One factor to consider is that we can't actually do the technique; we can't actually break an arm, so we have to simulate and tell each other "If I did this, you'd do that". Grappling arts don't really have such restriction, the technique has to work. Of course, they can't break an arm either but they go to the submission point.

I ask seminar participants what the opposite side of a technique is and they usually show me the left-handed version that technically is the opposite side. What I want them to see is the attacker's side, their motion and reaction. I want to see the punch, the hands going to the eyes when poked at, folding when kicked in the groin, hands moving to cover the parts that hurt, etc. Huk Planas said the techniques work off pain and realistic reaction. He added that if you have a great partner to work on you will look like Godzilla Unchained when you work. It's choreography. Nothing looks worse than a partner who just stands there while you do the technique, waiting for their turn.

Instructors act as the third person when watching application. They see what needs to be corrected and what's being done well. They get the attacker to try to do a follow-up to demonstrate points such as cancellations, weapon formation, accuracy, timing and if the student has put their partner in a loaded position where they can launch further attacks (a function of cancellation angles is to prevent that).

I took the idea of the third person and presented ideas on what to do if the third person needs to be defended, rather than what they are seeing, as he wanted us to consider and work on. It's What If? stuff, what I call going into the laboratory. I create scenarios in which you are with a child, a spouse, a date or even a stranger. There are no prescribed techniques for these, so you have to take elements from your basics and technique sequences and apply as needed. It's Parker's formulation phase, based off of work in the What-If phase. I liken this to common emergency procedures we all have done. A fire drill is an example. We posit that a fire has broken out. What do we do? Options include evacuation, getting a fire extinguisher, pre-planning an evacuation meet point, and more. It's been thought out and practiced. This is the same. Talk with your children about what to do if there's a fire. Talk with your spouse about how you'd react to a street situation. One of my black belts and his wife were approached by a man wanting a cigarette, since he'd seen my guy smoking. That's a "hook", a reason to make contact with a target, which bad guys do. He was given a cigarette and the man then asked for a light. Again, a practice used to maintain the contact with something else in mind. He got his cigarette lit and then said he was hungry too. This was part of the chain of actions which may have led to forcibly attempting to get money. However, our man told him he could smoke that cigarette or eat it. End of contact. Who knows what the man's decision tree looked like, possibly the following?

Choose target and then:

- Ask for cigarette. Possible responses are "Don't smoke", "Go away" or get cigarette.
- On to the next target or get confrontational? Or get cigarette then, either move on or ask for light.
- Move on after getting the light or ask the next question. Watch for reaction.
- Ask for money or food, or money for food.
- Get money/food or told to go away.
- Leave or get confrontational.

It may be worth talking with your partner about their actions should a fight break out between you and another individual. Ask, or tell, them not to get involved by grabbing you, which happens a lot. Most people don't like fighting and don't want to be close to it. Some will try to intervene in a variety of ways, a common one being grabbing their partner to stop them. That can result in getting struck by the other party when they take advantage of your disadvantage. Have a plan, like you do for a house fire.

You can see how this works. Apply it to your own experience and develop solutions. Working in downtown San Antonio I had a lot of contact with homeless asking for handouts. One told me she was hungry, so I took food out of my lunch bag and gave it to her. I turned away and heard it hit the ground. I asked her if it wasn't good enough and she immediately displayed anger and cussed me out. I believe she didn't want food, she wanted money. And that's generally what I've been told by those who work with such people. Homeless have also verbally threatened my life, so I don't take contact with them lightly. I do sympathize with their life but I also consider how they got there and know that many of those I had contact with were not interested in the shelters and available resources. I opt out.

Keep in mind what I wrote elsewhere in this book that cameras, phones and bystanders are third person eyewitnesses. Your actions in an altercation may be captured. Be judicious in your responses, verbally and physically.

Embryonic to Sophisticated Basics

An embryonic basic is one that has one move and one effect. If you shuffle, the one move gets you from one point to another. That would be embryonic.

A sophisticated basic done with one move but has dual or more effects. A shuffle in which you not only move but also make contact with the opponent's leg, causing a disturbance or buckle, is sophisticated. (Master Key move.) We can also call this a double factor, but it's not necessarily pointed out as such when we talk basics.

These are basics we have refined from initial instruction and "get more for our money", as Mr. Parker said. He'd say, "He got more than he bargained for. How can he squawk?" His techniques showed us how to get the best results from simple moves.

When we step back into a stance when grabbed from behind in a bear-hug, we not only establish our base (Rule #1) but by using a reverse bow stance in which we straighten our rear leg and use the extension to snap the back of our knee against the front or inside of his, we get a balance disturbance and possibly a leg sprain or break. The net effect is base set, opponent off balance. Two-for-one. Another effect is in play if we've checked his hands by pinning and struck the groin with a hammerfist as we set. So we've added back-up mass to the strike and this becomes more an example of double factoring because we're combining upper and lower body with the effects, not just one move. It's a distinction but don't get caught up in that. There are sometimes distinctions without differences.

In other techniques we might step to stabilize, buckle a knee, and land on an instep as we rake the nose with an inward downward back-knuckle and continue its path to clear the arms while striking the nerves. That's a lot of effects for a primary move. The caveat here is that in trying to get the most out of a move, some seek to add even more. "Prefix the pin with an eye slice as you knee the groin, raking the shin as you step down into an instep stomp with the raking back-knuckle that starts as a hammerfist to the temple and becomes the nose break. Can you? Maybe. Should you? Maybe. The problem can become that you get in your own way. There can be too many things you're trying to make happen at once. Mr. Parker cautioned me about moves that actually detract from the effect due to this. There are things advanced practitioners can do and beginners cannot. Yes, there is a space to put that insert in but not right now for the beginner. The system is taught in a way as to filter in such things as you advance and it's based on developing the desired effects, qualities and abilities beforehand.

Just as an embryo grows and develops, so do the basics. It takes time, a gestation period. I taught some basic concepts to children and sophisticated basics was one. I asked a class what that was and one child raised her hand and said "It's a basic that went to school." Yes, young lady, and I like to think it wears a tuxedo with a top hat and uses a walking stick. And maybe a monocle. Sophisticated.

Universal Pattern

Ed Parker's Universal Pattern is a multi-dimensional concept that is a type of mandala, very much like those in other systems. The simple version is shown by diagramming the eight basic angles of attack, which look like compass points, clock hand positions or a gunsight. I include it in these essential principles because he created and used it to get us thinking about using motion on multiple planes. It is an analytical tool. We wore the one-dimensional version on our uniforms as a shoulder patch, to be used as an instructional aid. We could trace out patterns for the student to help get the idea of a pattern across.

Thinking about multiple planes should help us see lines and paths of action, use of power principles, checking angles, points of view other than ours, bracing angles, considering What-If possibilities and more. If he'd have had the technology we have today, he'd have been able to show us the three dimensional version that he saw in his mind, which was a sphere shape. That's a concept others use as well. Some picture themselves at the center of that sphere, and when they step, it moves. It's very dynamic. I picture it, as I think many do, as being when we make contact, what might the possible follow-up angles be? A spherical Universal Pattern appears in my mind. I've found that looking at it like that it gave me a better understanding of what moves are possible and practical from a given position. Some moves are possible but not practical.

I had spoken with Mr. Parker about how I saw technique patterns in the air. He excitedly said that was how he saw it too. Years later I was told by a student about a statement made by SMA Joe Palanzo about me. He said "Lee Wedlake sees things in multiple dimensions simultaneously." I appreciate that being recognized.

We all process information differently. I've said to seminar groups that if we have forty people in the room, we are in forty different rooms. We perceive things differently. The room temperature could be felt as too warm, too cool or just perfect. Lighting, colors, mat surface are different for us all. Ed Parker did a lot of work to give us multiple tools to understand motion and the Universal Pattern is just one.

I was in college and there was a Jeet Kune Do class on campus, so I went to check it out. I approached the instructor, identified myself as a Kenpo practitioner and he went off on a lecture about how Ed Parker stole the idea of the pattern from the Indonesians. His rant attracted his class to us and he got so absorbed in it that when I walked away, he didn't even notice. Once again, I refer you to Parker's writing about the pattern. Go online and look up "mandala" and dozens of diagrams will appear. There's lots of versions, this is ours.

Web of Knowledge/Family Groupings

I see the Web of Knowledge and the Family Groupings as being two halves of a whole. The Web groups techniques by attack categories. The Family Groupings, later renamed Family Related Techniques, group techniques by response to the attack. Mr. Parker structured the system in such a way as to show opposites and reverses, and that included not only moves but concepts, principles and definitions. I think he built these two things like he did so many others, which was with the idea that if you didn't get it one way, it would be presented in another and you'd get that. He did it with disguised repetition in the techniques, with terminology and these models. The Web contains the attack, the Family contains the response.

His books show the Webs, so I won't repeat that here. His description of his inspiration is also there, so I'd have you read that. What I have students do is look at the categories and ask why they are set like that. It's easy to just accept them because that's what he devised but doing some thinking about them is illuminating.

We have, for example, categories of grabs and tackles, locks and chokes, hugs and holds. Ask yourself why you think he put grabs and tackles in the same category. Same with the others. You'll have to discriminate, like he did, the measure of degree and/or placements of the attacks as well as the force applied. Run your ideas past your instructor, you'll both learn something.

He classified the attacks as dead, semi-live and live. Again, "dead" refers to grabs. "Semi-live" are pushes. "Live" attacks are punches, kicks, weapons. I think it's important you understand this is a teaching construct to impart ideas. We know, as anyone who grapples knows, that grabs can travel. We also know that a push is really a heel-palm strike. We know you can do a push defense for a punch or vice-versa. The techniques are taught for given attacks as examples of ways to cope with it. Sure, we could teach every punch defense for a straight punch, but we don't. He laid it out so we'd see straights, roundhouses, hooks, uppercuts and overheads, as well as combinations. That would reduce response time since you're used to seeing them coming, recognize them and draw out your response. (You should try doing the roundhouse defenses for straights and vice-versa. It's part of the What-If phase.) As a whole, the system gives you ideas on handling a variety of attacks. There's such an array of possible attacks that instead of trying to have a technique for each one, we give you Master Key techniques and principles, and you select what's appropriate. (See the reference to Hick's Law elsewhere in the book, regarding how the mind works when there are too many options.) Grabbed by the wrist, you learn that going out by the thumb works best. Techniques teach ways to do that, dependent on the grab.

Family groupings, or family-related techniques is the other half of that aspect. The Webs give us the attack and the groupings give us the response. The model was changed from what I call a "Three Model" to a "Two Model" when presented in the *Encyclopedia of Kenpo*. When I first was introduced to it, it was 1) family groupings, 2) related techniques and 3) associated moves, those being the three model. Later he combined the first and second and it's known as 1) family related techniques, along with 2) associated moves, the two model. It has been my experience, when teaching advanced students, that some understand it better with one or the other model. I start with the three model and switch to the two when I see them struggling with it. This is also an example of his flexibility in thought and action, applied to instructional technique.

The classic example of a family grouping was *Dance of Death, Thundering Hammers* and *The Sleeper* techniques because they all started from the identical position. The step forward, the block and the hanging arm were the same Point of Reference, as was the Point of Origin. It exemplified the concept he was teaching.

But if you read his definitions, which changed a bit over time, they include those two terms, which means the family is not limited to relating them by those three factors. I posit that when you step forward or back and use a left neutral bow stance with the left inward block, the rear arm position does not have to preclude the technique as being part of the family. Therefore, any of the other techniques starting with the inward block, regardless of footwork or rear hand position, would be in a family. I believe that's why he changed the term from Family Grouping to Family Related Techniques.

Students ask questions about all this. How many groupings? What constitutes a family? How many in a family? I don't think there's a fixed number and a number was never mentioned to me. I believe that YOU set the number. The end result of this idea is to get you to understand the structure of the system and be able to use it. We all think differently and if I tell you it has to be some number and you don't see that, you probably won't accept it and it will never be yours. These don't fit in nice, neat categories as so many of us would like. And psychologists will tell you that trying to get things to fit neatly can be frustrating and frustration leads to quitting, quitting in the sense that you'd stop the analytical process. Two can make a family. Many cultures center on family and structure things like a family. Our ranking systems does it. Sifu means teacher-father, for example. Chinese systems have older brother and uncle titles for senior practitioners. Call it a chain of command, if you like. Parker's Hawaiian heritage was built on Ohana, the family. And he told me that the techniques have that aspect to them. Little brother (a block, maybe) is in the fight and other family members get involved (opposite hand, kicks, etc). The whole family supports.

A family can be only two. So if you're looking for more in a family, maybe there just are not any. And if there's just one, it's an orphan (his term). We all know there are techniques that just don't seem to fit/relate, those are the orphans.

You may consider related techniques as the ones that look a lot like whatever technique you chose as the head of the family. I think *Five Swords* and *Circling Wing* have a strong family resemblance. In my mind I see a family grouping. You may prefer to see them as family related techniques. Doesn't matter, it's what makes sense to you as long as you see a reason and purpose to the relationship. Your groupings will change over time as you see things differently. I read an example about relationships (non-Kenpo) and six brothers were described. When together, you could see the family resemblance. Individually, you'd see one had a beard, another a mustache, another had both, etc. But they are still brothers. The same with looking at techniques. If techniques follow what I call a gross physical pattern, recognizable even to someone with little or no experience seeing them, I'd group them.

Everything is related. All the techniques have stances, blocks, parries, strikes, etc that you could relate. Same DNA, just like every human on our planet can be related. Minor things, like these all have a right back-knuckle, may be useful but probably not. Yes, the back-knuckle is shown to different targets with varying timing and all but it's the sequences that give them meaning. I advise you look for those to build relationships to. If you understand this you can point out that this sequence is used inside, the same one outside, in a different zone, another with the opposite foot forward and another alternating the arms. It brings new meaning. Ah! Look at the many ways a sequence can be used. That inward/outward elbow sequence to the head in one technique is shown in another but inside the arm and on the ribs. It's shown in another technique outside the arm, and still hitting ribs. That's just a start.

If the sequence is not there but you can relate in another way, it's an associated move. You might see a combination that strikes with the hands and another that hits the same targets with the feet, it's associated. The technique, *Bow of Compulsion,* strikes the inner knees with the hands. The extension to *Hooking Wings* does it with the feet. Same pattern, same targets, different weapons. Oh, so you can essentially do the same thing with your feet you did with your hands? Yes, Grasshopper. And you can do it on an opponent who is on their back. That's in another extension. If you're unfamiliar with what extensions are, lower rank techniques had endings to them. You might see the base technique as a half technique, or an unfinished one, though still effective. The endings are a way to show other ways to move, they have timing, weapon and target changes and show how to use them on an opponent in a much different position. You might even use the extension portion as a stand-alone technique.

You should get a much better understanding of the structure of the system when you go through this exercise. You will see the how the points of origin, timing, methods of execution and more are demonstrated. In general, if you hear "It's just like…" it's probably not. Certain movements are identical to others in various techniques. Dropping back in a neutral bow stance and then transitioning to a cat is "just like" movement in multiple techniques. But the arms are doing something different, so "just like" should be qualified. I think the duplication of such examples of motion being described as associated moves gets you to dig deep and see what's really important.

Point of origin/reference

Mr. Parker used the terms point of origin and point of reference in his explanations of the Family Grouping/Family Related Techniques construct. They are both important for understanding family groupings and angles/methods of delivery.

We know he labeled motion by point of origin and taught, as an example, hammering and thrusting methods in executing an inward block. One was done from a hands-high position and the other from hands-low. They're shown in Short Form One and you should have been taught those from a horse stance, too. Looking at techniques being grouped by point of origin is therefore helpful. You might decide to group techniques that start with a thrusting inward block. You might get hung up on whether you stepped forward or back with it, whether it's inside a right or outside a left, but know that if you just look at the motion, your list will change. The reference points are different.

The eye-opener for beginners is they will see that same right inward block can be used inside a right punch attack or outside a left. Now we're back to Master Keys and Hick's Law. Newer students will typically do that human thing of listing "everything they know" by attack. They'll show you a list they created that shows all the punch defenses in one list, kick defenses in another, etc. It's the appropriate start point for making sense of what they're learning. Advise them to do the What-if work and see if what works inside the right works outside the left, and what kind of left, and so on. Instructors can point those relationships out to get them on their way but we have to let them do the homework. I think a good starting point is in the yellow belt techniques. The first self-defense technique uses a right thrusting inward block inside a right and the second uses it outside a two-hand push (really outside a left). That's repeated later in other techniques, both inside and outside (the point of reference) and they'll see the footwork change, other positions and uses of the rear hand and more. The formula is presented and carried forward.

Overkill vs Over-skilled

The Parker system is noted for its fast, explosive hand techniques. What stands out are the self-defense technique applications with multiple moves. Watching Kenpo demonstrated in its longer sequences generates either "Wow" or "Why do you need to hit them 16 times?" The Karate principle of "One punch, one kill" is important. I believe Kenpo should be done with each move intending to be done as the only move. Ed Parker's teacher, Professor William K.S. Chow said if in a street fight it went past four moves you were losing. So why the long techniques?

One – the techniques are ideas; simulations, and give the student information on possible answers to attacks.

Two – multiple moves apply the Margin for Error principle. If that first punch, which was intended to put a smoking hole in their ribs missed or they absorbed it, you are trained to continue. Hence the Over-skilled part. This does not mean you are required to do the entire sequence on an opponent in the street. As I teach in seminars, just because you can do something does not mean you have to do it.

Your training should impart a sense of awareness under stress and allow making appropriate assessments and decisions "on the fly". It may be hard to justify in court why you broke their arm, poked an eye or fractured the spine because they grabbed your lapel when a lesser response may have sufficed.

You must have situational awareness in a high-stress situation and not just go off on the attacker. Should it go to court the standard of what a reasonable person would have done will be applied to your case. You will need to know what is necessary to do.

ED PARKER AND THE WRESTLER

I was told this story by Mr. Parker. He was in a large city, I believe he said New York. There was a news story about a woman who had been murdered and numerous people had witnessed it, with not one of them calling the police. Why? All of them said they "didn't want to get involved".* Mr. Parker was scheduled to have breakfast with a famous wrestler and when the met, they talked about the incident. Parker asked him what he would have done. The man answered that since he had a wife, children and a house, and that he was a professional fighter he would not have intervened. His reasoning was liability, he could lose everything. When he was asked by the wrestler what he would have done, he told me he said, "I'd have gotten in, taken care of business, and disappeared". Knowing him and hearing other stories about him from seniors, this is very much an Ed Parker thing to do. In today's world, disappearing would be extremely hard to do, with cell phones and surveillance cameras being everywhere. I go into this a bit more in another chapter. This sounds like the murder of Kitty Genovese in New York. It's a famous case.

Application Principles

Stages of learning, variable expansion and more

Ed Parker's International Karate Championships (IKC) logo incorporated a flame as part of the design. The flame has three points, with the highest being centered. It symbolizes the stages of learning, those being primitive, mechanical, and spontaneous.

Primitive indicates the primary stage. It is when the student is first learning the basics. I see primitive as being what an untrained person would do, such as flailing with punches, like a child would. Mr. Parker looked at it as being refining of motion, organizing it for fundamental usage. He likened it to speech, when one learns to pronounce letters and words phonetically. For us, it's standing in a horse stance and doing full-range hammering inward blocks. That's Ed Parker's "sounding out" the primitive movement.

Mechanical indicates the stage at which one works by-the-numbers. You'd see Short Form One as being mechanical. Parker describes it as the stage where a student is better able to describe a move than use it. He says there is more thought involved than knowledge. The how is done in the primitive stage, the why is sinking in during the mechanical stage.

Spontaneous indicates the highest level, represented by the flame's highest tip. There's little or no thought as action begins. Think about spontaneous combustion with a fire starting. There's little start-up process, it bursts into flame. It's not "Oh, he's throwing a right punch. I will step in and do Five Swords". It just happens. Of course, this is after the cues, the initial approach and confrontation and physical action occurs.

Three Phases – the ideal, What-if?, and formulation phases

Mentioned elsewhere, the ideal phase is the set situation we use to teach a technique. We tell people they are ideas on how to handle an attack. We have more than one answer to an attack, so we have more than one technique. Will one work for multiple situations? Yes, those are Master Keys. However, Parker, in his analogy to the alphabet (the English alphabet), told us some letters are used more than others and if we needed an X, for example, we are glad we have one. Letters represent sounds and some sounds are also used less than others. You get the idea. In this case, if we need an alternate response due to position, range, the attack angle, etc, we have ideas already presented to us in the ideal phase, which should allow us to respond faster. That technique you think is a bit odd is an X.

I think that since we have 154 standards and some have a lot of moves, we get criticized for a number of reasons. How do you remember them? Do you need all those moves? What's wrong with a simple block and punch? Memorization is good, especially as we age. *(It's been shown that the following is good for us as we age. Physical exercise is necessary and it's better if it involves <u>complex motor skills</u>. Kenpo is better than walking. <u>Memorization</u> is also beneficial, as is <u>doing things in a group</u>. Look at the groups doing Tai Chi in the park. It's <u>exercise</u>, it requires memory and it's complex movement, done in a group.)* Do all the moves on the attacker? We only do what's necessary but we are armed with ways to handle it if more is needed. There's nothing wrong with a block and punch. I think each move in a technique should be done like it's the only move. If I stop you with the block, that's a good thing. If I have to do two moves, that's ok too. We really don't plan to do all twelve moves of *Dance of Death* on someone. Many of our ideal phase techniques are really What-if scenarios.

He called them What-if?, because a student would often ask "What if he does this?". The process of using this phase is important, vital actually. It should start with taking a basic technique and asking what else it works for. You think and you experiment. You learn what you can and cannot or should not do. The process is expedited with the guidance of an instructor. As you learn more advanced material you see the ideal phase is actually a What-if. What if you stepped forward with the other foot and did the same side hand combination? What if they blocked your initial counter? What if they pulled instead of pushed, or simply stayed static? Many of the techniques teach these variations but also leave more to be explored.

This will lead you to phase three, the formulation phase. You know that in everyday life we say we have to formulate a solution to a problem, or an answer to a question. You formulate a response to the attack using what you have learned based on the experience you have gained. That experience can be general life lessons, mat time and/or real-world street experience. Openings (opportunities) present themselves and you exploit them based on knowledge of many factors.

I learned about Margin for Error in Kenpo, although it's a common term in English, but I ingrained the concept. When I learned to fly airplanes, I saw the same idea used in many situations. I dealt with a crosswind on landing and thought I needed margin for error to safely handle drift caused by the wind. I used the technique I was taught and positioned the airplane on approach so that if I was blown sideways a bit, it was manageable. Same concept, different arena. That's what I mean by taking other experiences and applying them.

In this phase we have other terms in use. They are variable expansion, fighting formula, and grafting. To make an analogy to food, when you formulate you start with a recipe and substitute other ingredients. We start with a move or moves, then we apply the idea of variable expansion using what Parker called a fighting formula. We alter the pattern we were taught, when necessary, and expand the technique. How we do that is by using a prefix, suffix, adding a move, deleting a move, inserting a move, rearranging the moves, altering weapon(s) and/or target(s) and regulating speed and/or power. The recipe (ideal phase technique) called for a block, chop, eye poke and an uppercut. You instead did a parry, a back-knuckle, heel-palm and a claw. You altered weapons and targets. You regulated the amount of force by using a parry to redirect instead of a block. You could take the four moves and rearrange them, possibly doing the block last if he punched later. Mr. Parker did a drill he called the Four Factorial, using four moves and rearranging them, resulting in numerous combinations. You have to take time to experiment with this and it pays off.

Grafting is a bit different. The term is common, we hear about skin grafts in which skin is taken from one part of the body and used at another. Gregor Mendel is often credited with being the first to use grafting with plants to study the resulting variations. He's the father of modern genetics. We cross-breed techniques to come up with a third technique by grafting. You start with an ideal phase pattern and graft or add-on part of another ideal phase pattern. We've all done it. We started with one technique, the body went on auto-pilot, and we ended with another technique, seamlessly grafting one onto the other. It's not wrong, it's a good thing because you recognized a body (arm or leg) position and just kept moving. But you were able to do that because you learned the standard pattern and got the idea of what to do. Instructors have to know the standard techniques to transmit them, students need them for the information and demonstrate it. So don't beat yourself up if you grafted or did a "change-up".

Margin for Error

Parker's Kenpo stresses Margin for Error. His definition from his early work, the *Accumulative Journal* follows.

"The execution of a defensive or offensive move which, when delivered, gives you greater latitude to work with in the event of error or miscalculation."

Readers should know that his art evolved over time and that included the terminology. Later writings would enhance this definition. I include this here to give a sense of what he was intending. A broader application encompasses the thought that defensive and offensive moves include alignment, foot and body maneuvers, timing and more. Fighters of any system will tell you not to over-commit with a punch, for example, because if you miss you are not in a position to recover and follow-up.

Figure 7: Over-committed.

From body positions to angles of delivery, the principle is in place. He wanted his student to be able to act from any given position effectively, whether with the footwork, hand positions and body position. Delivery of an upward block is an example. From a horse stance, we chamber as we do with a punch, at the ribs. We throw the block up the center-line, as if delivering an uppercut. It can be a block or a punch. A points along the way, it may need to become a different block or strike. Say we went to stop a right overhead attack and it changed to a roundhouse punch or they used the other hand, the margin for error position allows us to use a different block efficiently.

A related principle has us use such a movement in one of three manners. This example uses the motion as a block (defensively). A second application is to use it as a strike (offensively), that uppercut I mentioned. The third would be to use it as defensive offense, using the motion to break an arm that has grabbed your lapel. There is no need to change angle or method of delivery to be effective in one of the three ways, though the final angle might vary. The block would be more over your head while the arm break would be more forward.

It might help you if you visualize the intersection of the eight angles, as shown on the Parker crest (the "gunsight") and looking at where you could go from that central position. You'd have to picture it vertically, horizontally and diagonally and on different planes to get started.

Checking

In the system we position ourselves, as he defined, to "hinder, restrain or repress an opponent from taking action." We are not unique in this but it does stand out. You don't often see the rear hand chambered at the hip or ribs as in many Karate systems.

There are essentially eight ways to check along with numerous variations. These include checking by:

- position (such as a guard)
- pressing (putting pressure against an opponent's elbow when defending against a punch to keep it from folding and removing your teeth)
- pinning (pin the arm, leg or body against something)
- hugging (much like the previous but with more body surface contact)
- grabbing (self-explanatory)
- sliding (moving from one point of body contact to another, such as down an arm from shoulder to wrist)
- striking (check the weapon, limb or body by hitting it)
- burdening (dropping weight to hinder movement such as sinking with an elbow strike to the opponent's spine and leaving it in place).

One will find references to other types of checks, over twenty of them. These are largely distinctions in magnitude or duration of the check. Some hit harder, some keep the contact longer. Others are merely another name for the same thing, such as burdening check or gravitational check. Still others are repetitive names. I see no difference in a detaining check versus any other check as all checks detain. It's in their overall definition. Like the term "contouring", "checking" is an overarching term with both having several sub-types.

A principle associated with this is having a rule guiding you to know where your check goes. Parker wanted the practitioner to be self-correcting and one needs to understand the principles to do so. When checking, the general rule is "Strike high, check low. Strike low, check high".

Figure 8: Strike low, check high.

Figure 9: Striking low with a check too low.

An elbow to the head would dictate we cover our ribs. Placing the check above the elbow would make no sense and chambering at the ribs or hip might expose us to intentional or unintentional counters. It's that floating hand position that triggers questions from those unfamiliar with the idea, usually because they are used to seeing that other hand chambered. While Kenpo, Filipino Martial Arts, Wing Chun and others teach checking, this does not mean others are ignorant of it. I'd hazard to say that nearly every system checks in one form or another, putting up a guard, covering up, etc. We know the body reacts to impact in certain ways and that such reactions can cause us to be struck in one of two ways; the intentional and unintentional. Our checks are placed to handle the intentional such as a follow-up strike, and we position ourselves in anticipation of unintentional reactionary positions, like a leg that rises when the opponent is falling, potentially striking us.

Placement of checks has caused discussions about the slapping seen and heard when Kenpo practitioners execute a technique, both on a body and in the air. This subject has been endlessly discussed in books, articles, online discussions, etc and I suspect it won't ever go away. The slap was described by Parker as being useful for 1) timing. It's often coordinated with footwork and that "slap", when done solo, coordinates the two. 2) Authoritative application. Again, when done solo, it looks like you're slapping yourself needlessly but in application it is used as a pin to keep a hand(s) in place so it can't be used intentionally or unintentionally. In grab defenses, that pin helps get the opponent off balance when we step-back, the timing I refer to above. 3) It has potential to be used as a parry on the way to the pin and possibly as an insert strike. Now the downside. It's often done incorrectly in some instances, the practitioner simply hitting themselves for effect. The slap itself positions the hand incorrectly. Slapping requires you put the palm of the hand on your body which does not afford the ability to ward off or grab well. I think it's been perpetuated because students see and hear their instructors do it and imitate by slapping, when the "thump" a properly formed and placed check makes goes into position. A check at the ribs would be done with the thumb side and wrist making contact, fingers up. The sound is less but if you are aping, slapping is good enough. Be aware of where, how and why you might hit yourself.

White and Black Dot Focus

This is a concept married to checking. I initially had a hard time remembering which was which until I figured out that we're black belts, we use black dot focus, as a memory aid.

Parker used this as an illustration of what he thought were the two types of focus, barring the definition some use when describing delivering a punch and "focusing" its energy on a particular spot. Focus here meant awareness.

Black dot focus is intended to give us a mental image of a black dot on a white background, representing total awareness of things other than the strike. It is an allusion to checking. We don't pull a hand back to the ribs if the other is needed to check. That indicates we are aware the opponent's elbow may bend and strike us.

White dot focus is represented as a white dot on a black background. The black symbolizes being unaware (can't see in the dark, I suppose). He wrote that it emphasizes power, not protection.

*It's interesting that the definition changed from the original, which said it was a Japanese concept of focus. In the *Infinite Insights into Kenpo* glossary in Volume 4 it is changed and says one visualizes a white dot on a black background which represents unawareness. The word, Japanese, is omitted. I submit that in his early years in Southern California's karate scene which was dominated by Japanese stylists, and when he was labeled a rebel and told his art was not pure, he had a bit of an attitude. Maybe he softened or got politically correct and decided not to point at them.

Multiple attackers

There are 10 standard two-man techniques in the system. These demonstrate his ideas on handling multiple threats, both simultaneously and sequentially.

I redefined, for myself, his terms of dead, semi-live and live in this context. A dead attack, as he classified them, are grabs. We have five techniques used against grabs by two attackers. A semi-live was described as a push. Punches and kicks are live attacks. The way I see it we have to consider that categorization as a teaching construct, used to get a student familiar. New students are most likely to be uncomfortable and unfamiliar with punches directed at them. Make the attack dead, and the student is likely less apprehensive. When they are more at ease learning is facilitated and confidence increases. We know grabs can travel and pushes can strike. The dead hand can move, as it does in grappling. We know that a push is actually a strike. A double heel-palm to the shoulders is a push but also a strike. That established, we find defenses for combinations of a grab or hug and a punch attack. I call those hybrid attacks semi-live because one is dead and one is live. The remainder of the two man defenses are for live attacks. These would include punches and approaches, as the ideal phase techniques were taught.

There are four components to be considered in practicing these techniques.

1) Hit the first person, then the second, go back to the first and again to the second.
2) Get out of the middle.

3) Finish with the opponents on 45° angles to you.
4) In practice, when one person moves, everyone moves.

Of the 10, five of them are for grabs. Two are for a rear bear hug and a front punch. One is for a rear grab and front punch and the last two are for a front punch/rear approach.

The grab defenses are side shoulder grabs (three of them), one is for side grabs on your arms and the last is for grabs from the front and rear. The breakdown is 80% are for side attacks and 20% for front/rear. Of the three side shoulder grabs, two are at arm's length and one is for close in. The defense for grabs on your arms is as if you're going to be taken away. The last is for grabs at 12:00 and 6:00. (It's a gaseous state technique, moving three directions at once.) It is up to the practitioners to explore the What-if phase of these and look at how they could be applied if the attacks are on angles or are hybrids, such as a front lapel grab and a double grab on one arm (12:00 and 3:00, for example). None of the ideal phase techniques show handling those angles but are easily adapted.

Of the two bear hug/punch combination attacks, which are a "You hold him, I'll hit him" attack, one is arms free and the other arms pinned. Both deal with a punch from the front. What to do if the bear hug is such that you have one arm free?

Of the remaining three, two are "free" or "live" attacks. The front attacker is punching and the rear is approaching. Both of these have you move toward the front attacker on the first move. Why? Because you can, and since the second is in the obscure zone where you can't see, you will need distance, which equals time, to sort this out. The third technique steps back because the rear attacker has grabbed you, at the collar or shoulder. If you attempt to step forward (purposeful defiance, you may be thinking), the rear man will likely pull you back and possibly off balance. It's safer to step back, establish your base, and strike. Once again, you back in the laboratory and experiment with the attacks from different angles. This is also where you will find the change-up points in the techniques, particularly for the kick combinations. You'll see that a combination in one technique easily substitutes for the standard sequence.

These 10 were originally in the 32 green belt requirements. Green belt was considered the footwork rank. This is where the kicking combinations, sweeps and combination sweeps were taught and/or emphasized. It's also where you learned the five knife techniques and the rest of the combination punch and combination kick defenses. One major premise he had was you'd spent much time developing strong stances and punching ability, so it was time to get those legs moving. You would get the chicken kick variations both front and rear as well as crossover kicks.

- Chicken kick – front leg, rear leg (this one has you switch sides, you'll end with the opposite side forward
- Chicken kick – rear leg, front leg
- Rear chicken kick – front leg, rear leg
- Rear chicken kick – rear leg, front leg
- Back kick, front kick – same leg kicking
- Back kick, front kick – alternating legs
- Front kick, back kick – same leg kicking
- Back kick, front kick – alternating legs
- Crossover kicks include front, side, rear and roundhouse variations
- Sweeps – a front roundhouse and reverse roundhouse combination, a 360° spin sweep, a front roundhouse/spinning buckle

This list is just to get you thinking.

1) Hit the first person, then the second, and repeat.

I don't have to tell you to hit hard and fast. The presumption is that you are outnumbered. They may have more than the two that are active, may be armed, and you may be disadvantaged by having a second person, or more, that you have to protect, those being children, a partner, significant other or even a stranger.

Looking at what the techniques have us do as initial moves we see chops to the throat, kicks to the knees, claws to the face, and a variety of strikes to the groin. These are vital areas, also called anatomical weak points.

Note: The Encyclopedia of Kenpo gets repetitious with much of the terminology. You'll find several "see also" entries and this is the case with these two terms. Sometimes there are up to four terms for the same thing. Why? I believe the major reason is that he knew that not everyone gets it with the same explanation, term or demonstration. So he gave us an option to use alternate terms. As for why more than two, I have my speculations.

These strikes cause a lot of pain, can crush a windpipe, cripple joints, slice and poke eyes to limit vision, break a nose and possibly cause one to lose the ability to procreate in the future. As I write elsewhere, just because you can doesn't mean you should. If you chop #1 in the throat and he drops, you probably should not return and do more damage. The technique considers that you may miss or not get the desired effect, which forces you to position yourself and decide whether you need to strike again. Lawyers, judges and juries will apply the "reasonable person" standard to your actions. Fighting is illegal, and in today's world what you are doing will probably be captured on video. If that video shows you dropped him, or both of them, then went back to continue retaliating, you're probably going to lose your case. Situational awareness is key and knowing the physiological and psychological responses to stress will affect what you do in what may be perceived as a life-threatening situation. You will have to be disciplined enough to know when to stop. Read up on the OODA loop (and other decision-making acronyms). Created by US Air Force pilot, Col. John Boyd. He created this for fighter pilots.

- Observe
- Orient
- Decide
- Act

It's a loop, and you and the opponent's each have one going constantly. And you have to know when to stop acting. Video may or may not capture sound. I recommend loudly voicing that you don't want to fight, and your posture should reflect that too. Use a position that is good for protection but doesn't look like a fighting stance. It's hard to defend what you did when the audio plays you saying you didn't want to fight but the video shows a full-on fighting stance. And if there's no audio, all they see is that stance.

2) Get out of the middle.

Two basic ways to get out of the middle is to move forward or back, or to pound your way out. 30% of the techniques move ahead or behind the attackers. The other 70% strike them to create space.

Falcons of Force[1] gets you out by essentially spinning out forward. *Snakes of Wisdom* and *Marriage of the Rams* move you back as you initiate your counter. *The Bear and the Ram* gets you around and behind the rear opponent, *Reprimanding the Bears* gets you stepping back into him to buckle him, primarily because your arms are pinned and motion is limited. So, your motion is more in-place than the others. *Courting the Tiger*[2] moves you from side to side as you strike to separate them, making space. In *Grasping Eagles*[3], you stay in-place then move forward to strike them. *Gathering of the Snakes* has you outside their left punch moving forward and then using the front opponent as a shield, getting him between you and the other opponent. *Parting of the Snakes* has you duck under the front punch, then pound your way out on the 12-6 line. *The Ram and the Eagle*[4] has you step back, then forward, both counters working inside the attacker's arms. This one also has a shove element to it but it does that to move opponent #1 away while you deal with #2, while the previous technique shoves them together.

[1] Also known as *Opponents at Sides*
[2] Also known as *Kung Fu Wrist*
[3] Looks like *Stone Warrior*
[4] Also known as *Whirling Blades*

To recap. Move forward to back as to not be sandwiched. If you elect not to, use gaseous state motion to strike in multiple directions at once, as a gas expands to fill its volume. Use an opponent as a shield, force them together or create enough space to be able to work.

3) Finish with the opponents on 45° angles to you.

Don't do a great sequence, then put yourself in a position to be grabbed or struck. Just as we use a cross-out at the end of a single attacker technique and use the Angle of Departure to the Zone of Sanctuary, it's the same here. Historically, there were no cover-outs in the Yellow belt material. The original 32 Orange belt techniques only had three techniques that had a cover-out and they all ended with a kick. The 32 Purple belt techniques were taught with the single cover-out that was introduced in those Orange belt techniques. Blue belt and above all had double cover-outs

I have written about cover-outs in the past in other books and on my Vimeo instructional video pages. They were called cover-outs, cross-outs and even cross-outs on the cover by Mr. Parker. Regardless of the name they do four things; create distance, keep your center-line covered, keep your weapons cocked and allow you to scan for threats. The double cover-out provides a 360° scan. The rule is you go out on the nearest 45° angle (the Angle of Departure) and that puts you in the Zone of Sanctuary. Use the + x principle. The Plus is the 12-6 and 3-9 lines, the X is the diagonals. Some call it lines and angles. Anyway, if he's on the plus, use the X and vice-versa. It keeps you out of the line of fire and they have to turn to reach you.

There's a running joke in my lineage based on a story I tell about a conversation I had on this with Mr. Parker. My observation was that I saw it as their being on 45 degree angles to my position. Mr. Parker said "No, they are on a T". I saw it as a V, he saw it as a T. I of course deferred to him. "Yes sir, it's a T." The end result is the same, use whichever you like. Just don't back into or trip over one of them.

4) All our techniques are intended to be interactive.

That is, the opponent should be reacting realistically to each strike and maneuver, not standing like a statue or manikin. These should look like choreographed fight scenes you'd see in a movie. One of my senior students, Bruce Meyer, tells his people, "You have to sell it!" I remember seeing an old Bruce Lee movie in which he fights over 20 men surrounding him, but he does it one at a time. That's not how it works. All of them could not effectively attack at once, there's only so much room to work with. Watch body cam video of police officers taking down a subject when multiple officers must be used. With more than a certain number they get in each others' way. Therefore, I tell students to work in such a way that when one person moves everybody moves. Nothing looks worse than opponents waiting their turn to attack. Several of the techniques are done, on the attack side, with a recovery by the attacker, who then re-enters. Maybe that chop to the throat didn't drop him, so he stepped back, reassessed and decided to step in again. That's a more realistic training approach. It will also provide opportunities to graft technique patterns, use Variable Expansion, and formulation.

This brings up a related discussion as to when to actually start the defense. Most attacks do not appear out of a vacuum, something triggered this. Certainly, some attacks are surprises. You've been ambushed. But most of the time there are indicators. Some are obvious; "What's your problem?" or "What are you looking at?" Others are not. Maybe an out of control person decides to attack others and you become one of them. You'll have to overcome the "I can't believe this is happening" stage that often manifests and GET MOVING. For example, I get students to start the technique when they first feel a hand on their shoulder. All participants should go into action. In the real world you'd have to assess the situation in a short amount of time before striking. You can't just strike without knowing the situation. It would be embarrassing to chop your mother in the throat. I was once at a crowded motorcycle event and walking along with a friend. As I stepped off a curb, I felt a hand grab my upper arm. I shook it off as I looked to that side and saw my friend stumbling. He said "You were supposed to help me." He'd tripped at the curb and intended to use me for balance. He had caught himself anyway but I apologized, saying I just reacted. The environment had me on alert and the grab was hard and unexpected. My point here is that you must react but using foot and body maneuvers are available as well as striking. It's context. I think many teach the techniques in a vacuum; there's no discussion of what, why, where, when this attack was precipitated. It's a "do this for a punch" without a why is he punching, where are you, is it sudden and unprovoked or was there a verbal altercation. Consider setting up the ideal phase techniques with a verbal component.

The techniques in which one attacker is on the approach raises a question. There are three techniques that were taught prior to the multiple attacker defenses in which the attacker is approaching from the rear (obscure zone). How do we know he or she is there? Here are some things to think about.

The aforementioned verbal component should be considered. Sometimes the bad guys talk to each other. That's one way you may know there is a second person. My father was confronted in a parking lot by a man with a gun. He'd gotten out of a car and demanded money. When my father, who worked in a hospital and was wearing scrubs, told him he didn't have any pockets and so had no money on him. The driver yelled at the gunman to hurry up and do the deed. The gunman turned around to tell him that Dad said he didn't have any money and that's when Dad took off running. The men were later arrested. Obviously, they were not professionals. So, there we have an example of the verbal tip-off. Related to verbal is sound. Did you hear something? A shoe scuffing the pavement, breathing, rustling of clothing? Look over your shoulder. It costs nothing and may buy you time and provide an opportunity to get a description that can be relayed to law enforcement. When I was in college and walking between buildings to go to class I did an experiment. If someone was ahead of me I'd scuff my feet or kick a pebble to see if there was a reaction. There are micro-expressions you can read and one is a person's head may turn toward a sound. I'd see that and what came after was very interesting. NOBODY turned to look at the source. All of them would start walking faster. I relate this story in my classes and seminars. Just take a look.

What about odor? I worked security in downtown San Antonio and we dealt with a lot of homeless. Some of them are quite fragrant and you can smell them a some distance. You'd smell them before you'd see them. It's a fact that women generally have a better sense of smell than men and that could be part of your early warning system. The smell does not have to be bad, either. A whiff of cologne may be a useful indicator.

Then there's your "Spidey Sense" (borrowed from the comic book, Spiderman). Something tells you someone is watching or something is not right. I read, years ago, that research starting in the 1980s showed a "morphic field" that connects organisms even when miles apart. What I read stated that it accounted for the sense we have that something or someone is present and watching us. Author Malcolm Gladwell, in his book *Blink*, refers to "thin-slicing". From Wikipedia:

"The term refers to the process of making very quick inferences about the state, characteristics or details of an individual or situation with minimal amounts of information. Research has found that brief judgments based on thin-slicing are similar to those judgments made with much more information."

The term was first used in 1992 and is now common in psychology and philosophy. All this points to what I wrote earlier about assessing a situation quickly and determining what to do. The reading I have done in texts on neurophysiology and neuropsychology make these points and validate my teachings. Research shows that female brains are more connected through the corpus callosum and accounts for the better sense of smell and what I believe is the classic "women's intuition". Gavin DeBecker, in his often recommended book, *The Gift of Fear*, tells women to go with that intuition and not dismiss the feeling. Morphic fields and thin-slicing are a real thing and should be included in the decision-making process.

Footwork

Feet go where they are needed. Years ago I had an article on footwork published in *Inside Kung-Fu* magazine. It's reissued in my 2025 book, *Further Insights into Kenpo.* Foot maneuvers were lower on what I call the *basics priority* list, due to having to manage the energy inherent in moving the mass of the body. These are taught as ideal or reference movements. A step-through forward or back is initially taught as moving from neutral bow to neutral bow, starting and ending with the same dimensions, just to get familiar with the name, movement, direction, contact with the ground, keeping the head height the same, timing, head/eyes in the proper direction and alignment, and balance required. We learn as we go this can be done starting and ending in different stances such as forward bow to forward bow (or almost any other stance), and that the dimension of the stance can be changed (start in a neutral, step-through, and end in a cat).

The listed basic foot maneuvers taught one how to <u>change lead sides</u> via step-throughs, switches and covers. <u>Maintaining the lead side</u> is shown in shuffles, which demonstrate doing so with timing and range changes. A step-drag shuffle covers less distance than a drag-step shuffle, while a push-drag shuffle changes the timing of a step-drag. The first moves the feet simultaneously and the second is a 1-2 timing. A timing change is also shown with a twist-through maneuver. While a step-through changes distance as it rotates ("distance with rotation", your shoulders and hips are turning in the process), a twist-through rotates, then changes distance, or changes distance, then rotates. Long Form One primarily uses step-through maneuvers, and they are repeated in subsequent forms, both forward and in reverse, as well as out of and into a variety of stances. Long Form Two shows the twist-through. I've written books with this information in them so I don't want to be repetitive, and I also refer you back to the *Infinite Insights into Kenpo* series. Quickly though, Long Form Two introduces the crossover (twist stance) three ways; front, rear, and in-place, (the rotating twist, which is the basis for the twist-through maneuver).

Other maneuvers are on the basics lists such as leap and jump.* Hop doesn't make the list but it is used in Form Five. These show timing, ground contact, and sequence changes such as launching from both feet and landing on both, launching from both and landing on one and launching on one to land on the same. Numerous other ways to adjust show up in both techniques and forms but they're not always obvious.

We prefer to keep our feet on the ground. Ed Parker told me we don't get into much sophisticated lower body maneuvering until the green belt level since by then you've developed a solid base and good punching power. The previous levels material included stepping forward, back, sideways and off-angling. The original 32 green belt technique requirements gave us single and combination sweeps, spins and spinning buckles and a variety of kicking combinations. He said that "kicks are exaggerated steps". A front kick is a step-through with the knee on a higher plane. A side chicken kick is an airborne front crossover.

While the foot maneuvers are at the bottom of the basics priority list, we learn them immediately as it is those maneuvers that keep you from being punched in the face. He told us that blocks were "physical reassurance", a back-up in case your foot maneuver wasn't done as desired. This raises another point. We step and walk every day. It's a skill learned as toddlers. It's how we step and walk that makes a difference. Some step lightly, others are stompers.

A word about basics lists. I refer to them as being listed in order of importance, or *priority*. The basics were listed for each belt level and Mr. Parker and I discussed the order he arranged them in. Stances first, because you need a base. Blocks next, because you should have a solid base beneath to be effective. Parries because they are a related redirect. Now you can counter-strike, so punches, then strikes, then finger techniques came in that order. Kicks and foot maneuvers were last, one due to the energy management involved and the other requires better balance along with momentum control, those being more difficult ones for beginners. Interesting that the original blue belt requirements did not have foot maneuvers listed but the green belt did. It skipped a belt.

Everyone's gait is different. Some of us, like dancers, seem to glide while others look like they stuck their finger in an electrical socket. We teach a stylized method of stepping and walking, all with specific purposes. And, as I have written elsewhere, we know that feet are stupid. They are the farthest from the brain and we will sometimes have to look down at them to assess what they're doing. Some students get the idea of how the maneuvers work, others are tangle-foot. I tell the story of Tiger Woods, arguably the world's best golfer. He decided to get a coach. His performance deteriorated, something many of us would not have expected. He has a coach, shouldn't he improve? No, he had to reprogram himself to a new method of motion. When he did, he was even better than he was when he was before. Peter Ralston, a world champion fighter from a Chinese system, wrote that we know how to throw a ball well enough but if we want to be professional baseball players, we need a coach. We coach our students with the maneuvers to raise them to a higher level. And what we instill in them can contribute to quality of life. They often report gaining better balance, improvement in sports and recreation activities and even fall prevention. I had a mother bring her son in for lessons and I saw that he was a "tippy-toe" walker. I taught him and later discussed that with her when I saw he was not doing it anymore. She told me the doctors wanted to do surgery to correct it and that what I taught him corrected the gait.

The associated body alignment, as I wrote in one of the previous sections, is keeping the spine straight. That does not mean it has to be vertical. Talking about standing positions, when we move, we don't do what Ed Parker called "jet lag". That's when, as you step back, your head stays where it is or even moves forward a distance. It lags behind the lower body. (OK, young 'uns, The term comes from air travel, often resulting in your body clock being off because you've covered a long distance in a short time. You feel like you're still back in the time zone you came from, thus "lagged".) That's bad because he was probably aiming at your head, and that's staying still or even moving toward the punch or kick. You can picture the result. It also puts the heaviest part of the body forward, which affects balance and creates an energy management issue. You have to engage muscle to straighten up and get the body moving back, in this example. Angle of No Return is a factor. It's when it makes more sense to continue in a direction instead of trying to reverse the momentum and go back where you started. You could "jet lead" as well, moving the upper body before moving the lower body. Combine this with what you may be wearing or carrying that adds weight. More upper body weight, like when you wear a backpack, can cause a "roly-poly" effect. I was cautioned early on when I was issued body armor, that was a factor.

Know about "extra steps" and "breaking the heel". Extra steps are seen when one turns a foot first, then does the maneuver, and readjusts that first foot again. You might see the front foot turn out in anticipation of the step forward, then the step, then the foot is re-positioned. Turning the front foot is unconscious and done to relieve some perceived bind in the leg but it also sends a message to the opponent that you're going to move (telegraphing). It won't turn out to the final position, so after the step, the foot is moved again it's re-set. That's a lot of motion to get the step done. Breaking the heel is usually seen when moving to the rear, usually from a forward bow stance. The rear heel rises, then the weight shifts back, then the step back occurs. The heel coming up transfers a bit of weight forward when you instead want it to go back. You should stick that heel down and step back.

Keep your head level when moving, don't bob up and down. Letting your center of gravity rise and drop opens you to being taken down, sends mass in the wrong direction(s) which reduces power transfer, and least of all, it looks sloppy.

My tai chi teacher told a story about the Grandmaster constantly admonishing a student to sink. The student did not take it as criticism, saying his teacher did it "because he loved me." There's an important lesson there for teachers. We correct because we want it done right but that's because when it is, it's efficient and it prevents potential injury, sometimes because of repetitive bad body alignment. There are instructors who teach because they get people to do what they say, not because it helps the student. I think that's a bad attitude. There's a saying, "Teachers don't do it for the income, they do it for the outcome". Slide your feet, keep your back straight, solidify your base (sink), relax your shoulders and breathe. You'll be fine.

The Four Ts - Tools, Timing, Targets and Travel

You won't find tools and travel in the glossaries but they are what I was taught early on. I first was taught three and I later added Travel to that short list.

Tools are your natural weapons. A man-made weapon also makes a difference but we're talking about the empty hand here. Timing is important because you can use the right tool at the wrong time. The Tai Chi school my teacher attended in New York was called the "Right Timing School". Being a Westerner, you might think that's a strange name for a business but it's not the name, it's a second name many Chinese studios use. It would be Mr. X School of Kung-Fu to outsiders, but known as The Right Timing School to those familiar.

Targets are the vital points, anatomical weak points and other areas a tool may be applied to. You can hit at the right time with the right tool and miss the target.

Travel is the distance the weapon moves before making contact. You must have the right amount of travel to be effective. Economy of motion is in play here. It's often misconstrued to mean that a shorter distance is better. If it hits and doesn't have the desired effect, it is not economical.

Let's look a bit deeper.

Tools

It's amazing how many ways the body can be formed to strike with. Open and closed hands, toes curled or straight, knees and elbows, even head, hips and shoulders. Descriptive labels were attached to the weapons related to their appearance or use. In English, we might know them as knife-hand, spear-hand, or chop. The hand looks like a knife and a knife can be used to slice or stab, as can that hand. Their path of travel contributed to a name, such as the crescent kick, which follows an arc. And the method of execution was also used, so we got snapping, thrusting and spinning. Parker coded many of the weapons in his technique names, doing what our martial art predecessors did, which was to provoke a mental image.

The principle of fitting weapons to targets is common. (Parker used it when describing contouring. See that section elsewhere.) As much as we like to use a screwdriver for more than installing screws, that's not its intended purpose. That's why we have chisels and scrapers, pry bars, etc. We use different tools for different reasons, one does not fit all. The same with natural weapons. Fingers are great for attacking eyes while a heel-palm is not. And heel-palms work well for hitting certain targets that a finger poke would not. We teach isolated basics to instill proper hand formation, which are the compact units and bracing angles, and the angles and methods of delivery. Then we integrate them into the self-defense techniques to supply ideas as to where to hit and when.

Speaking of when, timing is next on the list. It doesn't have to be next on yours, that's just how I list them.

Timing

Parker defined chi as mind, breath, and strength. Both the conscious and unconscious mind must be synchronized to use the chi (ki). Thus, timing not only consists of what the body does but the mind or spirit as well. One must time the upper and lower body to maximize force. It's the lower that sets the timing for the upper. You can punch fast but if the lower body is not used properly, force and effect is diminished. The timing must also be correct as to the movement of the opponent's body. If they are moving away as you make contact, effect is lost. The same is true if you move away as you strike. Too often we see strikes done as one is moving away. It may feel good in the air, but it just doesn't hit as hard. Using a weapon such as a stick, you can get away with it. As I wrote earlier about breathing, it's a key component. So, you have to hit with the right upper and lower body synchronization, as you move using the correct power principle and breathing and a mindset of having commitment to the strike. It can be disastrous to change your mind mid-strike.

Targets

There are vital areas that are prioritized in many threatening situations. Typically they are the eyes, throat, groin and knees. Can't see or breathe, lots of pain and the hinges that allow mobility are not working right, if at all.

Other targets are considered anatomical weak points, and there are a lot. They don't take a lot of force to injure. Noses, fingers and elbows, temples, the solar plexus and kidneys, liver, spleen, insteps and more are on that list.

Some targets are used to unbalance (sweep a foot), open other targets (push a shoulder to get at the chest), distract or even cover the eyes, rake a nerve to cause pain (shin kicks, rib rakes), and others take advantage of natural reactions of pulling back to cover (jam his own hand in his face or straighten an arm when the brain tells him to pull it back which results in two opposite commands and torn muscles, ligaments or tendons).

The technique applications teach these places to hit. It seems a lot of people don't know their own anatomy and won't admit it. Ask an adult where their solar plexus is and many just don't know. Please don't embarrass them, simply say something like, "You know, the solar plexus, right here" as you point to it. Often we're asked why something hurts and we can give a general answer but once in a while a "I don't know, I just know it hurts", suffices. But find out when you can, without going to medical school.

Travel

The weapon has to move a certain distance to have effect. That distance is called travel. All of this is a time/speed/distance problem. Bruce Lee was famous for his one-inch punch, which most of us can't do and if we can, it's hard to apply. The short distance effectiveness was a result of extremely efficient use of the kinetic chain from the feet to the hand.

All of us have to individually discover what positions we need to use in order to generate the requisite force. An instructor shows you what is essentially a general reference position to set up the strike. It's up to you to adjust it according to your body and its ability to hit hard. If you have a block that's too far forward and causing you to have to re-cock it to generate power, you have to pull it in to find the sweet spot. The instructor should be helping you with finding it. You'll have the right travel, using economy of motion and Angle of Desired Positioning. You'll be a dangerous person.

Recap

Is the weapon correctly formed? Is it being delivered at the right time to achieve the desired effect? Is it the going to the desired target and does it have enough travel distance to get the result we want? Make sure you have the right Line of Sight so you don't have to make extra, unnecessary, or unuseful movement.

Purposeful compliance and purposeful defiance

These are interesting terms. We know that compliance means to act or be in the process of being in accordance with a wish or command. Not doing that is defiance. Purposeful is important in understanding the term(s). If someone were to grab your hair and drag you and you have an unorganized response, it's not purposeful. You're complying due to pain and force. But if you go with it and utilize borrowed force to enhance a kick in the groin, that's purposeful. Borrowed force is using the opponent's energy (momentum) against them. It is not a power principle, as some think. See the section on body momentum. Many systems use this principle, Aikido comes to mind. You let them run into your counter. Borrowed reach is a related principle. It is simply a timing change. If he's too tall to kick in the face, you strike the groin to bring him lower so you can effectively reach him. If you strike as he bends, it's borrowed force. If he bends, stops and then you hit, that's borrowed reach. You "borrowed" reach by hitting the groin to reduce height.

We are grabbed from behind on our shoulder, so we step forward (provided we are not jerked back first), and this is purposeful defiance. In this context it is done to induce them to pull you back. The purpose is to work on their mind, that is, they grabbed you to keep you in place and you defy their wish. Most people would then pull you back to keep you where they want you. When they pull, you comply by going with their energy and deliver a strike. The borrowed force involved increases the power generated with torque. If we were to simply flail, again an unorganized response, it's not purposeful, it's merely reactive.

Some Parker Kenpo techniques roll with an incoming attack, dissolve the energy and give it back. *Triggered Salute* is a good example. Their push to the shoulder is used to contribute to your stepping forward (or back, if necessary) and delivering a heel-palm to the chin. Pure purposeful compliance.

Stepping in and blocking a punch is purposeful defiance. However, we also will use both in various situations. I gave an example earlier with the rear should grab. Another would be to have a grip on one of their hands and pull to get them to pull back. That would enable you to apply a wrist lock when you follow it. As SGM Parker said, there is an opposite and reverse for every move, principle, concept and definition.

In this case we get <u>them</u> to defy the action so we can comply with it and they help us do the lock. This push-pull idea permeates the system and is obvious in grab defenses. But you have to look at the attacks to see it. We tend to see the ideal phase techniques as stand-alone ideas. Looking at the What-if? phase gives us the opportunity to see the connections. For example, one of the handshake techniques is done when the attacker's arm is extended and another is used when it bends. (Basic joint locking ideas; you can lock when the arm is straight or bent.) Start with the straight arm technique and when they resist and pull back, go into the bent arm technique. Parker people, that's *Broken Gift* into *Gift of Destiny*. Both of those are stand-up jiu-jitsu techniques. Switching from one technique to another is called grafting or change-ups. It usually applies to when you do the standard patterns. If you do rearrangement, variable expansion, etc. it is a different animal and moves into the realm of the formulation phase.

Speed/Explosiveness

There are three types of speed. They are perceptual, mental, and physical. All three are defined in Parker's glossaries. Perceptual speed is how fast you take in stimuli and transmit that to the brain so it can make use of mental speed. Mental speed is how fast you process information and make decisions. Physical speed is self-explanatory.

There's a lot to all of this and I do not want to get into what little I know about neurophysiology and neuropsychology. I believe that what you need to know about are the important factors that affect speed. I make reference to such things as "thin-slicing" and the OODA Loop in decision making elsewhere in this book as well as some of my other texts.

The basics.

Everyone has a brain but they all work differently. Differences manifest in how information is collected and processed. I looked up the difference in the definitions of quick versus fast, words that are used interchangeably in everyday speech.

From www.writingskills.com

"Strictly speaking, *fast* is an adjective while *quickly* is an adverb. *Fast* refers to speed, and *quickly* refers to time."

"Slow talking doesn't mean slow thinking" is something I heard when I moved to the South many years ago. We tend to think someone is "slow" when they take what we think is too much time to answer something or when they just "don't get it".

Factors in perception and mental speed

We are not always at 100% performance. You're familiar with that feeling of mental fuzziness or "brain fog", in which you have problems, to a degree, with normal functions. You can't remember an often-used word or do some simple math. People rely on coffee or other drinks to sharpen up. It is often attributed to lack of sleep, lack of quality sleep, distractions, medication, illness, etc. Decision-making and performance is less than desired. You recognize it and takes steps to mitigate or correct it. You go back to bed, have another cup of coffee, discipline yourself ("Get yourself together!"), or get help doing what is needed (change, add, delete medication or ask someone to review something you're having the issue with). What if a situation develops while you're in this state? Response time is reduced. It may take longer to realize and accept what's happening.

Medication is often a contributing factor. There's a reason drugs have notes on them such as you should not drive or operate machinery while talking them. Some cause drowsiness, irritability, dizziness and more. Side effects run a scale all the way up to death. Just watch the drug ads on television and what they say possible side effects are, it's scary. And it's not just prescription drugs, over-the-counter medication does strange things too. Just try to know what they do, read the labels and warnings. When I was a flight instructor, I took a checkride with an examiner who told me he read the caution warnings in the Operating Handbook. That's the equivalent of reading the labels. All this affects collection of sensory input. Parker stated that environment included not was on or around you, but also in you. Who wants to fight after a heavy meal or when ill?

Then there are street drugs. This is scary stuff. Prescriptions can have some serious effects on thought process, reaction time, balance, etc. but at least they have been studied and approved (so they say). You can get a heads-up by reading the label or from a savvy pharmacist who tells you "Don't drink no booze". I had one actually say that. Street drugs are uncontrolled and who knows what reactions they may produce. Dosages vary, and they can have mixed ingredients ranging from harmless fillers to stuff that kills. Most of us can avoid or get away from the impaired person but some of cannot, we have to handle it for those who can't (that's your First Responders). Superhuman strength is often described as an effect of such drugs and subduing these people can be quite a task. My fellow Rangers told me they had a situation where it took six of them to get the person in handcuffs (and that they wished I had been there to help). Back in the late 70s I had a student who was a police officer and he told me a story of a violent suspect on PCP, which has an effect much like today's Fentanyl. He was totally out of control and fighting, they had to shoot him to stop him. He took six rounds of .357 in the chest, and he lived. It took enough out of him they could get him to a hospital and even so, when he was well enough to be jailed, he tore up the cell. Couple this stuff up with alcohol and mental issues, and it reinforces our advice to avoid fighting whenever possible.

Anabolic sterioids are an issue, too. "'Roid Rage" is a real thing. There are people out there who are not monitored in their usage of steroids. They use the steroids to bulk up in concert with their weight training. They self-inject and seem to ignore warnings signs. They are known to fly into a senseless rage and you could be the target of one. Street fights, gym altercations, road rage and other incidents are a result. All your typical preparatory considerations such as situational awareness and a mental preparedness to react with a plan should be in place.

Performance is affected by physical limitations as well. If one of your senses is limited or non-existent, the ability to receive information is compromised. If you can't hear, how do you detect sound that may tip you off to an approaching person? Two of my highest ranking black belts have limited peripheral vision, one due to a birth defect and the other as a result of stroke. They learned to accommodate for that and have done quite well. Sight accounts for a large portion of your sensory input and 70% of your balance information comes from vision.

My blind experiment

I go to Tucson, Arizona once a year to teach at a yearly event for Shawn and Rebecca Knight. I've been doing that for about since 2008. I've gotten to know a lot of people there, one being Dr. Bil Hawkins, a PhD who taught the vision and hearing impaired for about 40 years. He's a Kenpo black belt originally under Harry Hutchings and now with the Knights. Bil and I have had many conversations since meeting a few years back and he offered to take me out to experience what it is to navigate the world as a blind person. I finally got to do it this December of 2024. I have taken excerpts from our emails to make some points.

We met on a sunny Friday morning and after breakfast I put on a blindfold. I would be in darkness for three hours and have an unforgettable experience. I thought this was not just for me, as Bil believed, based on his taking Shawn and Rebecca through this previously, that it would provide insights that I could relate in my teaching.

"In all the 40 or so years of offering to show parents and teachers under blindfold what their child or student was experiencing, I've had three takers: Cullen Walsh's dad, a professor from the University of Guadalajara--and you. The Professor's area was brain research. She incorporated her couple of hours under blindfolds in her lectures for the rest of her career."

After all, we move ourselves through time and space using all our senses and this would bring a new and different perspective. I had the opportunity many years ago to work in a wheelchair and that drove home just what chair-bound people have to deal with, and I found that useful in teaching. I also felt that Bil was very curious to see what a 70 year old person with many years of martial art training would do under these conditions.

"To see someone of your age even consent to try this is pretty astonishing. At our age, most of our peers do not have sufficient balance,--without the use of vision-- that would even allow them to remain standing, let alone move safely."

I have done what most have, especially when we are young, to close my eyes and find my way around the house, to write with the opposite hand, and explore those sensations. When I teach Kenpo people about contouring I relate it to running a hand along a wall or shuffling your feet in the dark. This took it to a new level. Bil and I discussed the aspects of being born with low or no vision as compared to losing it later, such as due to an accident or illness. He dispelled the common notion that when you lose one sense, your others get better. Your brain processes input better, it's not that your sense improves. I have some hearing loss and tests confirm that. However, Bil told me that based on what we did that my hearing isn't really bad.

"Blindness is beyond scary. It is terrifying. Imagine a totally blind middle school student in the middle of those intersections at rush hour [the safest time because the patterns rarely vary]. But starting at about age 3...the buzzing sounds are information as valid for them as vision is to the sighted. You have many advantages: dealing in 3-dimensional space as a pilot, an absolute mastery of proprioception, and an uncanny ability to adapt within milliseconds to changing movement. A language capability to understand, structure and communicate to others...so, not exactly a tabula rasa..."

"If you ever have the chance to watch a blind person using their cane, you can watch how they use auditory and tactile cues to make decisions. As esoteric skill for a sighted person if ever there was one. There is also a myriad of YouTube videos for instruction in all these areas."

He drove us to a parking lot, a shopping mall and had me walking on straight and curved sidewalks, up and down stairs and ramps, and crossing streets. I was introduced to variations of sound and the sensation of using the feel of sunlight to help determine direction. I felt how wind can disorient you. It was intense.

"I was watching your problem solving strategies. You did some very bright things that I didn't usually see with a student for months, or years after instruction. I started with pre-school kids, so they were still going through the sensory motor phase, but with a cane attached. Including things not in the official curriculum: leaning over an edge of a building and spitting to hear how high up they were, counting "one-thousand...one...two..." until the splat. The problem was getting them to stop laughing so they could listen. And using water pistols to shoot at the engines of buses in the bus terminal [at the rear of the buses]. Some techniques were 'secret' so I didn't have them go home and say, "Mommy guess what Dr. Bil showed me today..."

"During the last phase of your lesson, I was looking for a particularly recurved sidewalk I used years ago on that part of town. Not really difficult, but the wind was going to be a disorienting factor. The barometric pressure was also dropping--which also serves to disorient...and totally discombobulate deaf kids. You never did panic. You were putting together what you knew from before and what you had

just learned [but had not yet fully integrated]. The thing to remember when losing orientation is 'return to the last true thing,' [which was facing the sun with it high on your left cheekbone.] The wind utterly destroyed the rational process--it was that third thing that bollixed up linear, logical thought. To be able to teach blind children, you have to have known that awful feeling of panic yourself."

At this point it was almost the three hour mark. I told Bil I was overloaded and just didn't know what my orientation was. I was apprehensive. He told me later how scary it was for him in his early training. I now have a much better understanding of what the blind deal with, daily.

"To see you employ your problem solving capabilities in an utterly different paradigm was beyond fascinating. And, as difficult as it was, you never gave in to panic. To suddenly obliterate 87-92 percent of your most useful sensory data and give it over to proprioception and tactile senses...making sense of the world with about 8% of your capability [before the decades of experience training you auditory sense to take over] is risky for the person and his or her safety."

"I got the sense that you saw the first hints of eidetic imagery and your brain constructed cues based on auditory and tactile information. I also saw you react to reflected and blocked sound. We begin to see that months into training.[a slight hesitation and a turning of your head to the cues]"

It was fascinating to internally look at my reactions, both physically and mentally. Toward the end I felt like I had a "picture" of the terrain I was on as if looking through night vision goggles. And when Bil guided me when I took his arm, the information one gets with a well-trained sighted guide through motion forced me to mentally let go of preconception, that is, the idea that we're going this way, even though I had almost no clue where I was. I wanted to cheat by keeping my eyes open even with the eye-shade to get any hint of light. I let that go early on and kept them closed the rest of the time. Bil would warn me to be careful removing the blindfold at the end, the eyes would be more sensitive. When Bil told me I tracked him, and also had me "find" him, was interesting.

"I thought of taking pictures during your experience, but I was concentrating on your micro-expressions and observing how you were sensing. Now and then I would walk past you [between you and the traffic noise] and you would slow just for a millisecond and sense the blocked sound."

"It was quite an adventure. That one investment in 3 hours of sensory deprivation affords you immeasurable opportunity to understand sensory integration. I also think it will provide you with anecdotes that will find just the right place in your seminars and teaching. As a writer and storyteller, you will include it in a story at just the right time to explain just the right thing in the right way to your many students."

Now I have a preview of what to expect should I ever have to live without sight and a deep appreciation for those who currently do. We know that many drills can be done in low/no light conditions or blindfolded. It increases sensitivity and is worth the time practicing.

Limbs

Missing and limited use of limbs and digits is also a factor. Long-time instructors have likely had students with one arm or leg, maybe even both. I've had wheelchair students and students with birth defects that severely limited their ability to use an arm. One could tell something was in his hand but could not determine its shape or texture. He was unable to punch with it but he could swing a mean horizontal forearm strike. Picking off a kick with an inside downward block was meant for him, too. He could do Kenpo.

I'd have students tuck a hand into their belt behind their back and work spontaneously. It's something you might have to do with an injured hand or arm. It makes you think. Working on your knees or sitting may also give you an idea what to do about limited leg and lower body movement.

A friend of mine, Charles Johnson, is a fencing coach and has produced Olympic level paraplegic fighters. A wheelchair-bound woman came to him after experiencing fencing at an event and wanted to learn. She asked if he could teach her. He told her he had no special training or experience in doing that but they could learn together. They did and she went all the way to placing in the Paralympic Games. A good coach can do that.

Age

No doubt we start slowing down as we age. Reaction time can be reduced, partly due to factors mentioned earlier. Flexibility is less in most but some of us can maintain pretty well. It takes discipline. Injuries over the years may accumulate and result in diminishing athletic ability. Some people just accept it at a certain age and go sedentary. Others, like poet Dylan Thomas, see it like this:

"Do not go gentle into that good night,"

Three men special to me embodied this. My father, Richard G. Stone, and Marc Rowe, M.D.

My father served in combat in two wars and as of this writing is about to turn 98 years of age. He has had a good run. He is a great dad and taught me a lot.

Rick Stone started with me at 68 years old, made it to black at 73 and went on to second degree. He passed at 91. He'd had four bouts with cancer and in 1979 had been told he had six weeks to live. While he came up through the ranks, he couldn't do a side kick above his knees but every one of them was done with proper form and power.

Dr. Rowe came to me in his early 80s for Tai Chi classes. He was on the verge of losing the use of an arm and a local doctor recommended he find a Tai Chi teacher. I worked on him and he had a "fertile, prepared mind", asked a lot of questions and practiced hard. He not only improved, but improved so much that by his mid-80s he set national power-lifting records in three events for his age group. So much for limitations. Mind, body and spirit work together and achieve marvelous things. Keep in mind that we have to change our training methods as we age.

Physical speed

Almost everyone is fast. That's what is called a "standard pattern", just like most people being right-handed. Some are faster than others. Everyone would pull their hand off a hot surface fast. However, there are people who have no tactile sense in the hand and actually wouldn't know it was hot. That's a rare exception. World champion Bill Wallace's left leg roundhouse kick was clocked at 60 miles per hour. He didn't look that fast on television, which was why I agreed to fight him in an exhibition match. Then I found it he really was that fast. A person like him has a lot of fast-twitch muscle fiber. Those are the ones that give us explosive, powerful movements. Biceps have a lot of them. Slow-twitch muscle fibers are the endurance components. Runners most often have a lot of them.

We experience different types of physical movement as we mature and some suit us better. We tend to select what we like and do that, often neglecting other methods. I think that's a good reason to try many activities, you'll probably find something you never thought you'd like.

We tend to classify partners in the studio as faster or slower than others. I've found it doesn't seem to make much difference. Coach them properly and they will get it figured out as to best work with their speed. It doesn't matter much if the slow person works a great grab and check to set up a punch and it works.

Explosive pressure, continuous weapons and flow
You've collected the necessary information, made a decision(s) and it's time to physically act. Your decisions include whether to act or not (verbal deescalation has not worked), number, size and type of attacker(s) (one or more, stature, male or female). Age is a factor. Younger people are typically stronger and faster. Will a heel-palm to the chest suffice? A slap? Or is a hard straight right the best option?

The Parker techniques are fast, explosive, have multiple moves and strike hard. They have been often described as brutal. Dr. Maung Gyi, a long-time friend of Ed Parker's once said, when seeing the techniques, "Eddie Parker very angry". Ed Parker saw Haumea "Tiny" Lefiti doing his art and adopted the speed and power he saw to ours. Our Kenpo was not done in the early days the way we do it today. Parker would make analogy to how explosives were used in the past.

In the American Old West, they'd plant a charge, make a line of gunpowder to the charge and light it from a distance. That took some time to generate an explosion. That's how he saw some traditional systems' execution of technique. Part two was how we learned to set the charge, connect wires to it and use a plunger system to send the electrical charge to detonate it. It was faster and how he saw many systems execute their art. He said he saw a James Bond movie in which a remote detonator was used for instantaneous result. That's how he wanted Kenpo done. You need to explode into a move. There's no wind-up and pitch.

Explosive pressure is the term he used to describe what you do once going into action. His techniques have us staying on the attacker, crowding them, causing pain (occupy his mind with his own injury), check the hinges (elbows, knees, spine/waist) to prevent or reduce movement and keep them off balance. This not to say you can't apply his fighting formula to this principle. Pressure can be increased, reduced, removed, applied asymmetrically, and in alternate directions. Once again, situational awareness is necessary so you can do what is needed, delete what is not, continue, stop, and justify what you do. See the section on overkill/overskilled.

Use of continuous weapons is married to this principle. While more traditional systems teach a "One punch, one kill" idea, systems like ours keep striking until we need to stop. (It's the stop part that is problematic at times. Emotions such as anger may drive us to keep striking past a reasonable point. I was taught as a child in a Judo school that the object of self-defense is to get home without being hurt. I add, that when possible, without the opponent being hurt either.) I wrote elsewhere that we should do each move like it's the only move, which is akin to the one-punch concept. I've hit men in street fights with one move and it was enough to stop them. I was cursed at but they stopped. I've hit men with multiple moves too, when the situation dictated it. I may have overdone it once, as I got a letter from an attorney telling me not to have contact with their client. I was young and foolish; emotion, ego, had gotten the best of me. I should have stopped at the takedown, but I laid a few extra shots in. The lesson is Don't Fight. It's said that if you fight, your chance of winning is really only 33% because you can win, lose or draw. In losing, you could be killed. In winning, you could kill some one and that is frowned upon, to say the least. Fighting is generally illegal. At times it's totally justified, which is the condition we operate upon with executing a technique on the street. And when we do we have to take into consideration the factors I have pointed out, and more. That can be very hard to do. Therefore, the default is Don't Fight. It can be very difficult to keep your composure in these situations. I cases where I have arrested someone, I have encountered individuals who will provoke, apparently hoping they could get an excessive force charge against us. I listened to absolutely horrible things said about me and my wife. Logic (no way he could know her and her actions) and training (using discipline and being aware of their tactics) allowed me to keep my cool. Afterward, myself and another officer admitted we'd have loved to punch him in the face. You can't do that to a handcuffed suspect. Well, you could, but it would not go well for you.

Minors/majors

Minors set up the majors. Majors are the "devastating impact" strikes. Picture a finger whip followed by a heel-palm. I think a whip to the eyes can be pretty devastating so we're back to magnitude, as referred to in earlier sections. Yes, a strike to the eyes is bad but in relation to the heel-palm, it's a minor. I was taught that minor/major means hard and harder.

Minors set up majors. The common back-knuckle, rib punch or jab/cross, inward/outward block combinations are examples. Either can have effect or do damage but it's the relative value that makes the distinction. I think that if you follow the hard/harder idea, you'll be better off. You don't typically do two minors simultaneously but we have examples such as the groin whips in the two-man technique *Marriage of the Rams*. Two simultaneous majors are more common such as in *Snakes of Wisdom* or *Destructive Twins*. Major is not limited to strikes. Two hard blocks striking the radial nerves can be damaging.

Majors are the big bombs. More depth of penetration is typically used. Even when considering an arm bar (lock) and an arm break, it's depth of penetration. The force progression is used here. If you just need to control them, you put the lock on and maintain as needed. Weapons or multiple attackers in the mix? Increase the force, go through the arm (depth penetration) and break it. I'd say that's a major.

When you're combining minors with majors such as with an inward/outward block combination, we refer to that as a double factor. There is more on this in another chapter. Consider major and minor in the context of injury. When discussing hurt versus maim with a student it became clear the distinction was not understood. If you broke their arm, eventually healed and regained its full use, they were hurt. If it is permanently damaged, it is maimed. Some of our techniques add insult to injury by re-breaking and/or twisting (wrenching, when combined with pulling). One technique has four sequential elbow breaks in it. These breaks are cataloged in the techniques to show the angles and methods and may be used individually elsewhere, not necessarily in that sequence application. Again, just because you can doesn't mean you should.

Tailoring

Parker liked to think of us as tailors, fitting a suit to an individual. He did not believe in the "one size fits" all idea. He would make examples in his seminars and books, often referring to taking clothing off a rack and choosing the correct size. We have to do the same thing with motion and sequence. Shorter people would have to put a shuffle in a sequence to adjust distance. The rule we use then here is "shuffles go where they are needed". Alternately, it's "feet go where they have to". The ideal phase techniques provide an idea of when and where to do so. I had a student with a bad case of arthritis and she could not do a half-fist formation. We found that a heel-palm suited her. The move was tailored due to limitation. So, many of the elements used in a technique can be tailored to be effective for the practitioner. I wrote in another chapter about such things as age, environment, limitations and more that highlight the fact that techniques must fit the individual instead of the individual fitting the technique. This is not a new concept in any style or system. It's up to an instructor (a teacher, really, there's a difference) to introduce and reinforce the concept.

Reactionary positions will force a change in a sequence. If your timing was off and the opponent bent more than anticipated, you'd have to alter what you do. Maybe you're forced to change the target, weapon, or amount of power used.

Speaking of power used, try regulating the amount of force between the two arms. We typically use the same amount with both. It's worth exploring to see how you feel varying the power in each limb during technique. Why do this? It's good just to try things to see if they're useful or not. And if you were in a situation where you had to handle an attack by a large man and have to maneuver your child or significant other out of the way, would you apply equal force with both arms? Doing so may jeopardize our partner. A hard block to stop a punch and equal force with the other to position them away may cause the lighter, smaller person to fly, which could be bad.

The tailoring principle is applied in his weapon work with clubs and knives. He specified what the length of a club or the size of a knife should be for use in his techniques. We often see a stick used in Form Seven that is obviously too long for the practitioner. The movements are a bit clumsy and even have a tendency to get in their own way. The stick he wanted used was measured by body proportion, as so many things are in our system. One end was to be at your palm and the other end one inch beyond that same elbow. It's not the standard stick that's bought from the martial art supply house. I studied Serrada Eskrima, which is a short stick system, very much like Parker stick techniques. I think of Serrada as the Kenpo of Eskrima systems – it's fast, close-range. I prefer it to the Parker material. As to the knife techniques as done in Form Eight, again we often see the wrong size weapon. Those are done best with a dagger-type knife, not the Kenpo fighting knife we see used. (That knife was designed by world-famous knifemaker and Kenpo black belt Gil Hibben for his black belt thesis in the 1960s. It is not easily manipulated in the ways prescribed in the form. It's a great knife, well constructed in all its variations and has what has been described as a "meaty" handle.) One has to consider the effects of actual use, which means blood on hands and weapon and how it slices or thrusts. Different blade shapes are intended for different uses. Blades with a belly cut differently than straight-edges. There are serrated, wavy, single-edge, double-edge blades and way more. Blood on hands can be slippery or sticky and the material and shape of a handle makes a difference. Sure, you can pick up a knife and start stabbing and slicing and that's dangerous. We have all been cut by something and know we need to avoid it. We also know that someone who is flailing away with fists can also be dangerous and need to avoid that too. It's all chaotic. If we're forced to deal with these emergencies, we become managers of violence.

"With" vs "And then"

Ed Parker was adamant about eliminating "and then" movements. He much preferred "with". He'd demonstrate compounded and simultaneous movements. In his Kenpo you see simultaneous strikes such as an outward back-knuckle with a vertical punch, one going to the head and the other to the body.

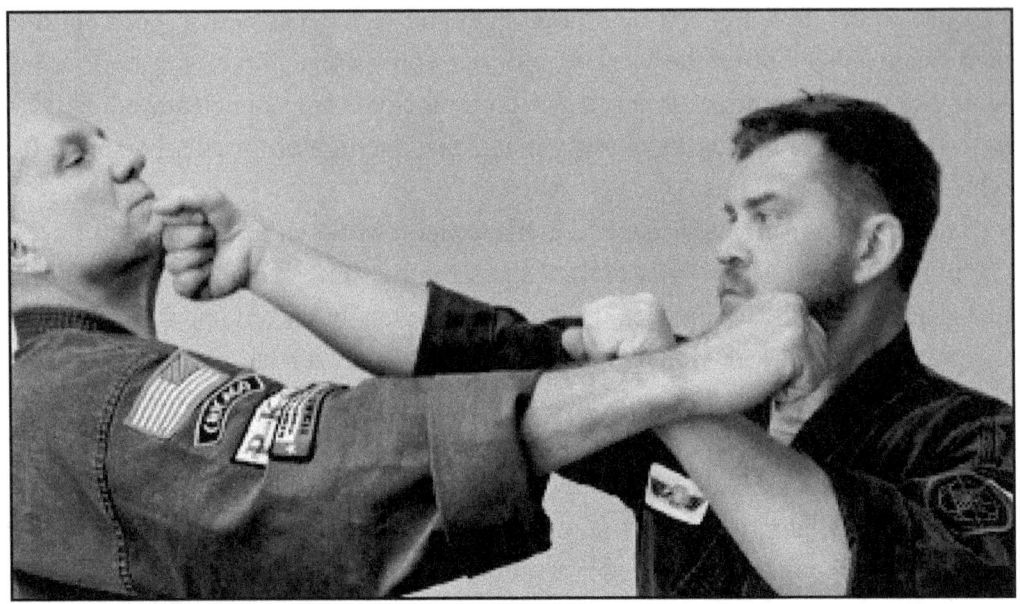

This photo shows a block with a strike, although the block would actually be a strike.

This employs not only economy of motion but a double factor, an open-ended triangle, and control of more than one zone at a time. Other examples abound.

"And then" is obvious when a practitioner executes in inward block, "and then" cocks it back to deliver an outward chop. We see it often in the first section of Short Form Two. Hang on, here we go. Defense side - if you were to have an application for it. The first four forms are basics forms and no particular attack is prescribed. However, most teach it, the first move of the form, as being used for a right punch. The block is delivered and often not in the best anatomical position for the practitioner. They now feel they cannot generate enough force for the chop, so they draw it back, cocking it. Cocking is what we do but not by using needless reverse motion, which this is. The block was too far forward or out, now somewhat over-extended and requiring re-positioning, which is the re-cock. The chop is now delivered as an "and then", that being you blocked "and then" re-cocked to strike.

Offense side – the attacker threw a right. What if they throw a combination right-left? The re-cocking hand is now traveling in the same direction as the second punch. We are no longer in position to block it. What if the attacker sees you re-cock and checks your elbow? You gave it to them and they took it.

You can argue that the sequence itself is "and then". Block and then chop. We show timing variations and the most efficient ways to do something. In this case it's that sequence. Other techniques would block "with" a strike. So what I'm describing here is needlessly adding an "and then".

Short Form Two is building on the principles shown in the One forms (see my book, *The Kenpo Karate Compendium*), and re-stating torque as the power principle. To really get some effect from that chop, you'd rotate your body, shuffle or drop. But you don't here. That's in Long Form Two and self-defense techniques like *Five Swords*.

Compounding is getting more effect in the same amount of time. One general rule we use is to take something with you as you cross the body. Maybe you chop right side of the neck with your right and follow through, drawing it back to your right side. Along the way you might rip with a claw or finger slice the eyes. That's compounding. It's also called an insert. Like many Parker terms, there are more than one for the same idea, which allows the instructor a choice in presenting an idea. If the student doesn't get it with one, they get it with the other. (If they still don't, well...)

As you have been reading, I'm sure you're seeing the connections between using principles. When we ask about what the principle of a technique might be, we are asking what the main one is, because many can be incorporated into a basic, move, or sequence.

Contouring

This permeates the system. You do this one Day One when you're taught to punch, being told to keep your elbows in, typically from the "chamber" position at your ribs, and follow your body contour, rotating the fist at whatever point you're taught. Mr. Parker told us some teach rotating the punch at different points during the delivery. Most start the rotation about halfway out. Others may tell you to wait until just before contact. He believed it didn't make much difference since the underlying principle of torque was unchanged. Doing so maximizes energy since allowing the elbow to flail or flap outward sends energy in a different direction than desired, that being the fist goes forward and the elbow goes to the side, thus dividing the energy and reducing impact. The lesson includes not only detail about punching (striking surface, targets, breathing, timing, alignment/bracing angles, etc.) but is an introduction to one form of contouring. Contouring is an overarching term, a kind of catch-all term. This first type of contouring is called guide-lining. We have Contouring as the head of the category. The two main sub-divisions are guide-lining and complementary angle. Guide-lining follows body contour with contact, following a given line of the body without contact is a complementary angle.

Sub-categories such as fitting, threading, needling, etc. abound. It can get confusing and that's why I like to keep it simple. I'd like to touch on the important ones. Fitting is included in the glossary of Vol. 4 of *Infinite Insights into Kenpo*. Other terms such as threading and needling are not. They don't appear until the 1992 publication of the *Encyclopedia of Kenpo*. That book was completed after he passed. In fact, none of the terms are present in his *Accumulative Journal* which has copyrights of 1970. I think it shows how he was always thinking and re-thinking his work. However, I feel it got a bit unwieldy by the time we got to the *Encyclopedia*.

We've already established that you can follow contours with or without contact. A sliding check is an example of following their body to move from one point of contact to another without losing contact. That's guide-lining. (Look at the section on checking, keeping magnitude and duration in mind.) In many techniques we follow an arm to a target by paralleling it. That's complementary angle. There's usually a head at the end of every arm, so it's hard to miss if you follow the line.

An important term is Fitting, that is, fitting the weapon to the target. Mr. Parker would later refer to this as the "Puzzle Principle". Akin to pieces in a jigsaw puzzle, your weapon can "fit" a target. Rounded weapons fit rounded targets such as a heel-palm fits a chin. Flat weapons fit flat targets as a punch would fit the sternum. Another example is shown by striking the groin upward with a reverse handsword instead of a reverse hammerfist. The original version of Circling the Horizon was done with an underhand reverse hammerfist to the groin. It was changed to an upward vertical reverse handsword ("ridgehand") because it fits the target better. Using the reverse hammerfist (the thumb side surface) tries to fit a square weapon into a triangular area, the crotch.

Positional Contouring, I feel, is important too. It's the reason we use our forward bow stance the way we do. Most systems position their front foot forward to 12:00, while ours are on the angle. The Parker reasoning is that should an opponent make contact with your leg and try to track it up to your groin (as we would, given the chance), that angle would deflect the attempt. It's a position check but illustrates that sometimes we follow a line to attack or defend. There's a pose initially shown in Form Four that highlights this concept. It "frames", and parallels body contours with the message being that we can use this idea offensively or defensively.

Object Obscurity is related to contouring in that we follow our own striking limb with a subsequent strike. We may execute an overhead claw to the bridge of the nose, which inflicts damage that likely causes them to close their eyes, so we keep that weapon in place to obscure the vision as the second weapon is being delivered. That overhead claw is often followed by a vertical back-knuckle (like an uppercut), the punch being in contact with the back of the claw on its way to the target, the claw being retracted as the punch strikes the target. The lesson in such examples is that not only can we guide-line our own body for a single strike, like the punch we earned as beginners, we can use the principle for multiple strikes.

Weapon principles

The Parker weapon defense principles are divert, seize, control, disarm. He referred to them constantly. Of course, they apply to other situations, but not all of them. I offer you could interpret disarm as being the mental aspect of the situation, getting an opponent to submit, thereby "disarming" them.

Divert

These techniques assume, as do all techniques, that you are unable to de-escalate or escape and are forced to handle the armed attack. Divert here refers to blocking, parrying or checking an attack. It includes "force against a neutral force", which is shown in the gun defenses. The gun being held and pointed at you is a neutral force. Blocks oppose and parries ride force, so you don't really block or parry the gun arm. You check or strike it. The moves look like parries or blocks and we use the terms to get the student to do what is desired. You have to divert the attack so you don't get clubbed, stabbed or shot.

Seize

Grab the weapon hand or arm if you can. Grabbing clothing works, too. Watch where you grab. Practice will familiarize you with what you need to be aware of. You don't want to grab the blade of a knife or machete. Grabbing a gun or knife, you need to know that the wrist can flex. Flexing the wrist with a gun may allow the shooter to pull the trigger and you get shot. We normally position our hands so we limit or prevent wrist action, don't get shot in the hand, are able to follow them when they naturally pull the weapon back when they realize you're trying to take it and possibly use it for some extra leverage on a wrist lock. We like to grab the hand and weapon, also to keep them from switching it to the other hand. With a gun, you have to watch where the barrel points. If they get a shot off, that bullet goes somewhere and you don't want it hitting a bystander. Maybe you're being mugged, you deflect the gun, it goes off and they shoot your significant other. Bad. Find a knowledgeable instructor who can show you the differences in revolvers and semi-automatic guns. You can grab a revolver in such as way as to restrict the cylinder rotation. Semi-autos, when the slide operates, can tear skin. Get educated.

Control

The previous paragraph described seizing and an element of control. If you are unable to grab to control, other methods are available. Striking and sliding checks are useful, especially when coupled with foot and body maneuvers. Staying in contact, using the open-ended triangles, gives you the best margin for error. Mr. Parker said "when you make contact, you're in love". Stay with them. This is used in the Filipino weapon systems. If you disconnect, it usually makes the job much harder. Control the weapon(s), and especially the zones. Just because you see a weapon and think that's the only one they have, doesn't mean that's all they have. Zone control keeps the back-up weapons away.

Pick off the right and keep them turned so they can't use the left (width zone control). Pull or push down so they can't kick or grab as with a leg pick (height zone control). Crowd them (depth zone control). Get control.

Disarm

Disarms happen one of two ways. You either make them drop it or you take it away. A strike to the radial nerve will often cause a reaction of opening the hand, and the weapon drops. Among other types of disarm, you can strip it out of their hand, forcibly releasing it. A division of attention would be called for, that being aware of where the weapon goes along with attacker actions. There's a tendency by both of you to focus on the weapon. You want to take it and they want to keep it. It can turn into a wrestling match, and often does. The flexibility in thought Mr. Parker spoke of includes knowing when to let go, possibly to switch to the other hand or go to controlling. If the weapon falls, you may step on it to keep it from them. If a knife, step on the handle, so all they have to grab is blade.* A gun can discharge. A club can be redirected, a flexible weapon like a chain can wrap. You're better off not being there. Bad guys do things like wield a sword, use stun guns, and way more crazy stuff. Sometimes a disarm just isn't going to happen. If it doesn't you're back to one of the other principles.

*If your luck is bad, it could stick in your foot. I've seen it happen.

If you grab it, hang on with a death-grip. If you're using it, generally the same. You can't or shouldn't do so with a gun necessarily because it throws off where the bullet goes. Knives and clubs, yes, grab hard. There is a time to relax your grip and you can't maintain the death-grip indefinitely. Point is, have a firm grip.

Thoughts on the combat mindset by Gary Ellis, 10th degree

Although not taught as a specific principle, Combat Psychology plays an important role in Ed Parker's Kenpo in the development of the Kenpo warrior mindset. This is quite evident if we take a look at the Forms as a good illustration of the underlying mental preparation of the student for combat.

Action is faster than reaction, so in a self defence situation we are already one beat behind our opponent (unless we are first to initiate the action) and so we must catch up and take control. Certain survival skills or tools are given to us by Mr Parker to achieve this.

In Short Form 1 the first move teaches us many important survival principles which start us on the road of developing the mindset of the Kenpo Warrior. At this stage the student learns to step away to gain distance, therefore moving the target before stabilising their base and shielding by blocking the incoming attack with a hammering inward block, in effect Beating the Action by Meeting it. A hammering inward block is utilised because our hands are held high in the meditation position prior to starting the form so Point of Origin is employed. We are taught to look forward and focus on the opponent, and to use the correct engineering and mechanics which ensure Economy of Motion. Timing, Breathing, Accuracy, Explosiveness, Determination, Guts, Fighting Spirit and Will Power all play a part.

We could add several more principles into the mix to consider. However the essence of the move is to get out of the way of the incoming threat by moving the target, gain distance and time, establish your base and shield yourself. Long 1 of course builds on this idea by showing how we can counter punch with the rear hand. The natural reaction of someone with little or no experience is to shy away and this is used to good effect on the first move of Short Form 1.

Short Form two psychologically flips this around and we step into the eye of the storm. By now the student should have a strong base and be well versed in blocking and punching, standing in a strong stance. (In the salutation we show the fist first before the open hand). This is a big step as we are now meeting the opponent's action with our whole body.

Short Form 3 and Long Form 3 close the range further and we are in counter manipulation range, in close using our elbows and short range weapons.

Form 4 introduces attacks by combinations of punches and punches and kicks thus again increasing the threat level and the psychological response.

Form 5 is the form of Destruction. Many of the techniques in Form 5 are killing and maiming techniques. This is the final stage where the warrior has to operate at a kill or be killed level. It is one thing to pull out a gun but can you psychologically cross the Rubicon and use it?

Through each form you are being psychologically prepared to be able to go all the way. That is why I refer to this as a War Art because ultimately it is kill or be killed.

To teach the Art properly with the mental attitude and preparedness to go all the way if you have to, ("Life or Death, Right or Wrong") it has to be balanced with moral teachings. If you raise the Tiger you must also raise the Dragon to control the Tiger. ("Warrior and Scholar must Unite and go forth into battle"). I link the three stages of learning also to training methods and the process of internalisation:

- Primitive: Thought, analysation, slow deliberate practice, focused action
- Mechanical: Feel, rhythm, timing, coordination, mechanics, breath and balance
- Formulation: Instinctive, fusion of primitive (thought) and Mechanical (feeling)
- Principles "Are" the Art. But they are useless unless employed effectively.

www.ingramcontent.com/pod-product-compliance
Lightning Source LLC
Chambersburg PA
CBHW051354070526
44584CB00025B/3755